Pulse and Digital Circuits

Sundar Srinvias Kuchibhotla

Assistant Professor
Department of ECE, PSCMRCET

Naga Lakshmi Kalyani Movva

Research Scholar, VITAP

Praveen Kitti Burri

Assistant Professor
Department of ECE, PSCMRCET

Acknowledgement

This textbook is the outcome of the inspiration that I received from **Dr.J Lakshmi Narayana**, Principal, PRIW, Khammam during his tenure as the Head of the Department, ECE, PSCMRCET.

I owe an enormous debt of gratitude to the **Management of Potti Sriramulu Chalavadi Mallikarjuna Rao College of Engineering & Technology, Vijayawada** without which this book would not have come into existence.

I am also immensely grateful to **Dr.K.Nageswara Rao**, Director, PSCMRCET and **Dr.K.Sriram Krishna**, Principal, PSCMRCET for thier inspiration and timely motivation.

I am specially grateful to **Dr.A.Ravi**, Professor and Head, Department of ECE, PSCMRCET for his encouragement.

Special thanks to my ex-collegues **K.Vijay**, **D.Suresh Babu**, **S.Pradeep Kumar**, **B.Mohan Swaroop**, **R.V.Shashank** and **T.Durga Prasad** for thier valuable suggestions and guidance.

Lastly, I am indebted to my wife, **M.N.L Kalyani**, for her love and support which helped me to complete the textbook even in hardtimes. I could not complete the book without the love of my sons- **Pranav** and **Dhanush**.

Readers can e-mail their opinions to **ksundarsrinivas@gmail.com**.

Sundar Srinivas Kuchibhotla

Dedicated to my mother **K. Nagamani**

Sundar Srinivas Kuchibhotla

Contents

PREFACE

The textbook PULSE AND DIGITAL CIRCUITS is written in the examination point of view. This book covers the following topics with solved problems

1. Linear Wave Shaping

2. Non-Linear Wave Shaping

3. Clippers

4. Clampers

5. Multivibrators

6. Time Base Generators

7. Logic Families

8. Sampling gates

Chapter 1

Linear Wave Shaping

The process by which the shape of a non-sinusoidal signal is changed by passing through a linear network is called Linear Wave Shaping.

The most important waveforms are sinusoidal, step, pulse, square wave, ramp, and exponential. In this chapter,response of High pass and Low pass for RC, RL circuits are explained.

1.1 Types of Non-sinusoidal Signals

1.1.1 Step Signal

It is a signal whose amplitude is zero for all t<0, and maintains and amplitude A for t >0.The variable A indicates the amplitude of the signal. The step signal is shown in the figure 1.1.

1.1.2 Pulse Signal

A Pulse signal can be generated by adding a positive step signal from t=0 and a negative step signal from $t=t_p$, where t_p indicates pulse width. The pulse waveform is shown in the figure 1.2.

1.1.3 Square Signal

The variable A_1 indicates the amplitude of the signal above the axis and A_2 indicates the amplitude of the signal below the axis.

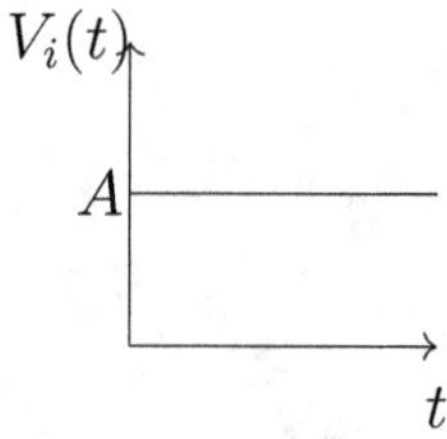

Figure 1.1: Step Signal

$$V_i(t) = A, \ 0 \le t \le \infty$$
$$= 0, otherwise \tag{1.1}$$

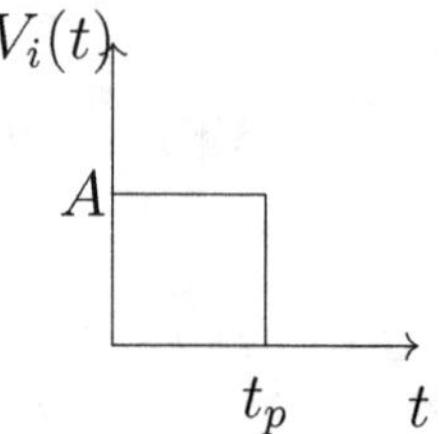

Figure 1.2: Pulse Signal

$$V_i(t) = A, \ 0 \le t \le \ t_p$$
$$= 0, otherwise \tag{1.2}$$

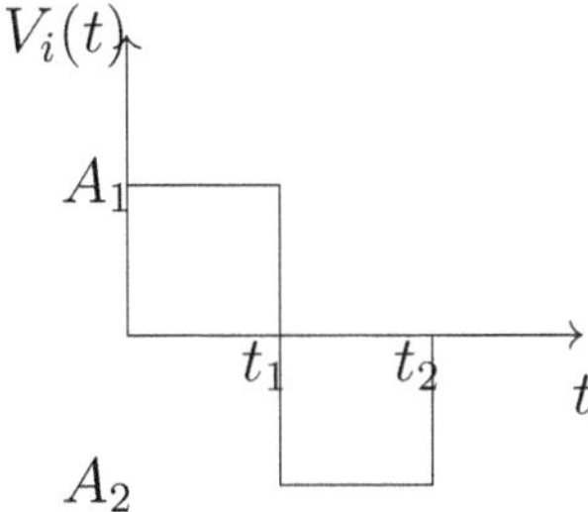

Figure 1.3: Symmetrical Square Wave

$$V_i(t) = A_1, \ 0 \leq t \leq \ t_1$$
$$= A_2, \ t_1 \leq t \leq \ t_2 \tag{1.3}$$

Square wave can be Symmetrical or Asymmetrical. If $t_1{=}t_2$, then the square wave is symmetrical, if not asymmetrical. Square wave signal can be generated by adding a positive pulse signal and a negative pulse signal. The symmetrical square waveform is shown in the figure 1.3.

1.1.4 Ramp Signal

Ramp signal is one where the magnitude increases same as time. The Ramp signal waveform is shown in the figure 1.4.

1.2 General Output Expression

Whenever an input signal is applied to linear network, output will be a transient and a steady state.

$$V_o(t) = B_1 + B_2 e^{-t/RC} \tag{1.5}$$

whereB_1 represents steady state output and B_2 represents transient state ouput. Substituting t as 0 and ∞

Caluculating $B_1(\text{t} \to \infty)$:

$$V_f = B_1 \tag{1.6}$$

where V_f indicates final output voltage.

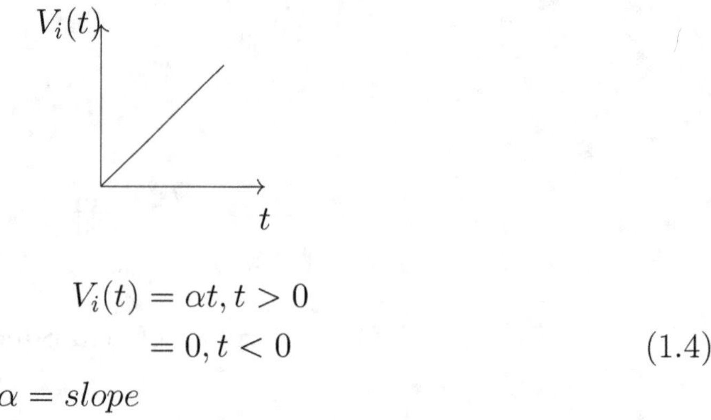

$$V_i(t) = \alpha t, t > 0$$
$$= 0, t < 0 \tag{1.4}$$
$$\alpha = slope$$

Figure 1.4: Ramp Signal

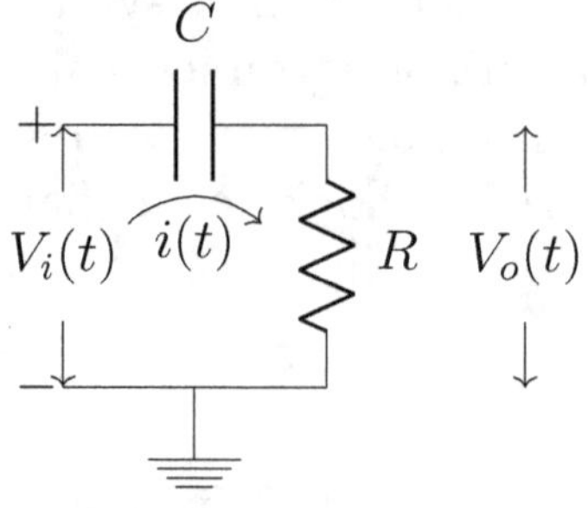

Figure 1.5: High Pass RC circuit

Calucating $B_2(\text{t} \to 0)$:
$$V_i = B_1 + B_2$$
$$B_2 = V_i - V_f \tag{1.7}$$
where V_i indicates inital output voltage.

Substituting B_1 and B_2 in general output expression

$$\boxed{V_o(t) = V_f + (V_i - V_f)e^{-t/RC}} \tag{1.8}$$

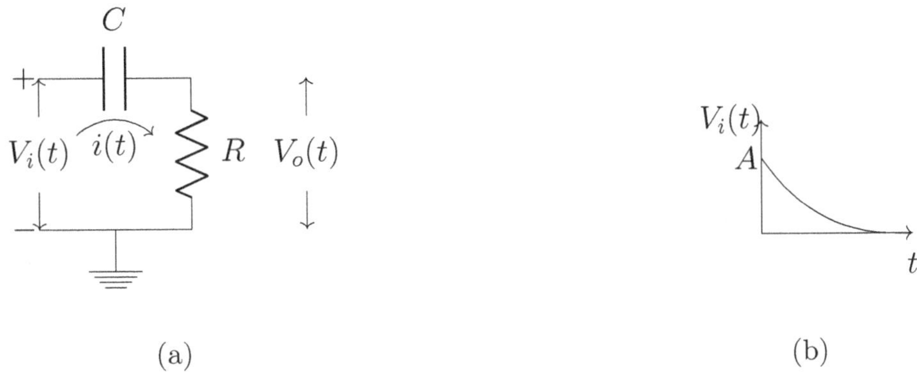

(a)   (b)

Figure 1.6: (a) Circuit Diagram (b) Output Waveform

1.3 High Pass RC Circuit

1.3.1 Step input of High Pass RC Circuit

When a step input signal is fed to High Pass RC circuit as shown in figure
1.5, the capacitor does not charge instantaneously. So, V_i=A.

As time increases, capacitor starts charging and it can charge upto the
maximum input volage i.e A. So, V_f=0. The output waveform is shown in
the figure 1.6

Substituing in eq,

$$V_o(t) = 0 + (A - 0)e^{-t/RC}$$

$$\boxed{V_o(t) = Ae^{-t/RC}}$$

(1.9)

1.3.2 Pusle Input to High Pass RC

When a Pulse input signal is fed to High Pass RC circuit as shown in figure
1.5,it's output wave form is shown in 1.7

$$V_1(t) = Ae^{-t/RC} \tag{1.10}$$

at $t = t_p$

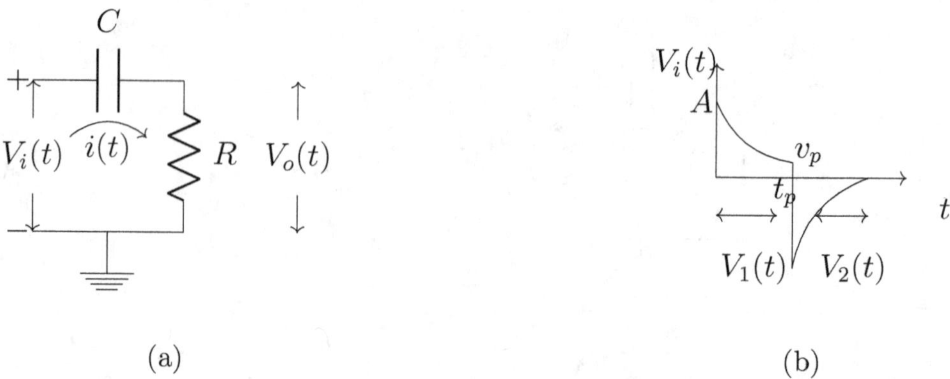

(a)   (b)

Figure 1.7: (a)Circuit Diagram (b) Output Waveform

$$V_1(t) = V_p$$
$$V_p(t) = Ae^{t_p/RC}$$
$$V_2(t) = V_f + (V_i - V_f)e^{-(t-t_p)/RC}$$
$$V_f = 0, V_i = V_p - A \tag{1.11}$$
$$V_2(t) = 0 + (V_p - A - 0)e^{-(t-t_p)/RC}$$
$$= (V_p - A)e^{-(t-t_p)/RC}$$

Problems

1. A pulse of 5V amplitude and pulse width of 0.5ms is applied to high
   RC having R=22KΩ and C=-0.47μf. Sketch the output and calculate
   % tilt.

   Solution:

   Given A=5V, t_p=05.3ms, R=22KΩ and C=-0.47μf. The output wave
   forms are shown in the figure 1.8

Figure 1.8: (a) Input Waveform (b) Output Waveform

$$
\begin{aligned}
V_p(t) &= Ae^{t_p/RC} \\
&= 5 \times e^{(-0.5\times10^{-3})/(22\times10^3\times(-0.47\times10^{-6}))} \\
&= 4.76V \\
V_i &= V_p - A \\
&= 4.76 - 5 \\
&= -0.24V \\
\%tilt &= \frac{A - V_p}{A} \times 100 \\
&= \frac{5 - 4.76}{5} \times 100 \\
&= 4.8\%
\end{aligned}
$$

$$(1.12)$$

Statement: Area of the output waveform in above the axis equal to the area of the waveform in below the axis.

   Proof:

$$\int_0^{t_p} V_1(t)dt = \int_{t_p}^{\infty} V_2(t)dt$$

$$\int_0^{t_p} V_1(t)dt = \int_0^{t_p} Ae^{-t/RC}dt$$

$$= A \int_0^{t_p} e^{-t/RC}dt$$

$$= A \times [\frac{e^{-t/RC}}{-1/RC}]_0^{t_p}$$

$$= -ARC[e^{-t_p/RC} - 1]$$

$$\int_{t_p}^{\infty} V_2(t)dt = \int_{t_p}^{\infty} A(e^{-t_p/RC} - 1)e^{-(t-t_p)/RC}dt \qquad (1.13)$$

$$= A(e^{-t_p/RC} - 1) \int_{t_p}^{\infty} e^{-(t-t_p)/RC}dt$$

$$= A(e^{-t_p/RC} - 1)[\frac{e^{-(t-t_p/RC)}}{-1/RC}]|_{\infty}^{t_p}$$

$$= ARC(e^{-t_p/RC} - 1)$$

$$\boxed{\int_0^{t_p} V_1(t)dt = \int_{t_p}^{\infty} V_2(t)dt}$$

1.3.3   Square Wave to High Pass RC Circuit

When a Square input signal is fed to High Pass RC circuit which is shown in the figure 1.5, the output wave form is as shown in figure 1.9. Assuming the square wave is symmetrical.Then, $t_1 = t_2 = T/2$ and $A_1 = -A_2$

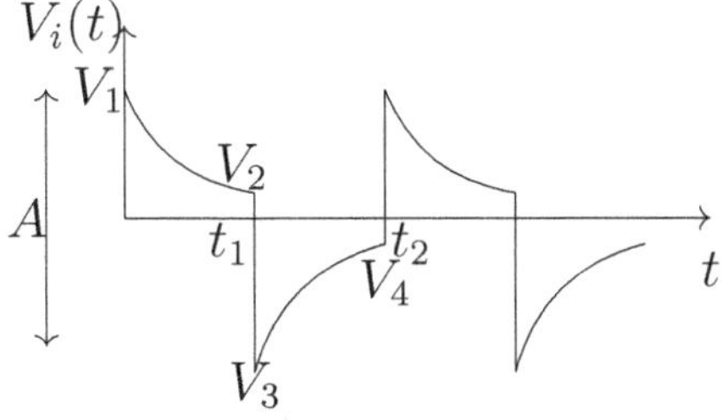

Figure 1.9: Output waveoform of High Pass Rc for a square wave input

$$V_2 = V_1 e^{-t_1/RC}$$
$$= V_1 e^{-T/2RC}$$
$$V_3 = V_2 - A$$
$$V_4 = V_3 e^{-t_2/RC}$$
$$= V_3 e^{-T/2RC}$$
$$V_1 = V_4 + A$$
$$since V_1 = -V_3, V_2 = -V_4$$
$$V_1 = -V_2 + A$$
$$V_2 = (-V_2 + A)e^{-T/2RC}$$
$$V_2(1 + e^{-T/2RC}) = Ae^{-T/2RC}$$
$$V_2 = \frac{A}{(1 + e^{-T/2RC})e^{T/2RC}}$$
\begin{equation}
\boxed{V_2 = \frac{A}{1 + e^{T/2RC}}}
\end{equation}
$$\boxed{V_1 = \frac{A}{1 + e^{-T/2RC}}}$$

$$(1.14)$$

1.3.4 % Tilt

It is defined as the change in output voltage amplitude due to the input
voltage maintaining a constant level.

$$\boxed{\% Tilt = \frac{V_1 - V_2}{A/2} \times 100}$$

$$\% Tilt = \frac{\dfrac{A}{1 + e^{-T/2RC}} - \dfrac{A}{1 + e^{T/2RC}}}{A/2} \times 100$$

$$= \frac{(1 + e^{T/2RC})(1 - e^{-T/2RC})}{(1 + e^{-T/2RC})(1 + e^{T/2RC})} \times 200$$

$$\% t = \frac{1 - e^{-T/2RC}}{1 + e^{-T/2RC}} \times 200 \tag{1.15}$$

Expanding, $e^{-T/2RC}$

$$\% t = \frac{1 - \left[1 - \frac{T}{2RC}\right]}{1 + \left[1 - \frac{T}{2RC}\right]} \times 200$$

$$= \frac{\frac{T}{2RC}}{2 - \frac{T}{2RC}} \times 200$$

since, $2 >> T/2RC$

$$\boxed{\% t = \frac{T}{2RC} \times 100}$$

Problems

1. A 2KHz symmetrical square wave of $\pm 20v$ is appiled to high pass RC circuit having 2ms time constant. Calculate and plot output waveform.
   Solution:

   Given: f=2KHz, RC=2ms, A=20-(-20)=40V

$$V_1 = \frac{A}{1 + e^{-T/2RC}}$$
$$= \frac{40}{1 + e^{-0.5/2\times 2}}$$
$$= 21.24v$$
$$V_2 = \frac{A}{1 + e^{T/2RC}} \tag{1.16}$$
$$= \frac{40}{1 + e^{0.5/2\times 2}}$$
$$= 18.75v$$
$$V_3 = -21.24v$$
$$V_4 = -18.75v$$

2. A symmetrical swuare wave is applied to high pass RC having R=20KΩ, C=0.05μf.

   (a) If frequency of the input signal is 1KHz and the signal swings between $\pm 5v$. Draw the output.

   (b) What happens if the frequency of the signal is reduced to 100Hz.

Solution:

Given: R=20KΩ, C=0.05μf, A=10v, f=100Hz

(a)

$$V_1 = \frac{A}{1 + e^{-T/2RC}}$$

$$= \frac{10}{1 + e^{-1/2 \times 20 \times 0.05}}$$

$$= 6.2v$$

$$V_2 = \frac{A}{1 + e^{T/2RC}} \tag{1.17}$$

$$= \frac{10}{1 + e^{1/2 \times 20 \times 0.05}}$$

$$= 3.77v$$

$$V_3 = -6.2v$$

$$V_4 = -3.77v$$

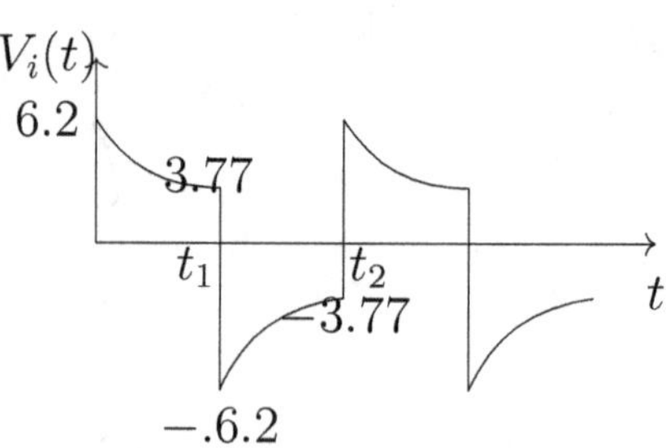

(b)

$$V_1 = \frac{A}{1 + e^{-T/2RC}}$$

$$= \frac{10}{1 + e^{-0.01/2 \times 20 \times 0.05}}$$

$$= 9.93v$$

$$V_2 = \frac{A}{1 + e^{T/2RC}} \tag{1.18}$$

$$= \frac{10}{1 + e^{0.01/2 \times 20 \times 0.05}}$$

$$= 0v$$

$$V_3 = -9.93v$$

$$V_4 = -0v$$

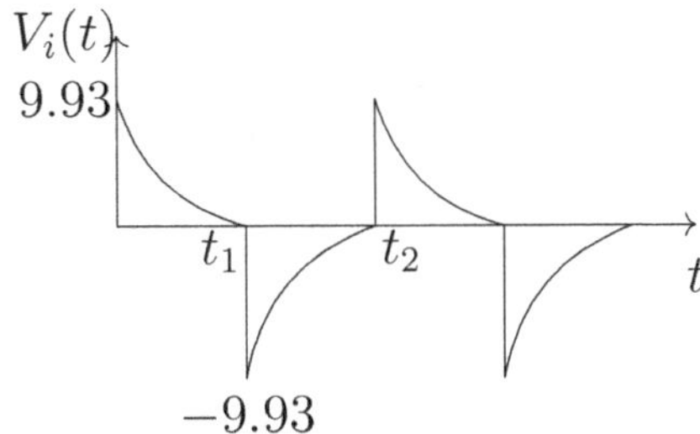

3. A 10Hz symmetrical swuare wave whose peak to peak is 2v applied to high pass RC whose time constant is 0.0318. Calculate % tilt.

Solution:

Given: A=2, f=10Hz, RC=0.0318, T=0.1sec

$$V_1 = \frac{A}{1 + e^{-T/2RC}}$$
$$= \frac{2}{1 + e^{-0.1/2*0.0318}}$$
$$= 1.65v$$
$$V_2 = \frac{A}{1 + e^{T/2RC}}$$
$$= \frac{2}{1 + e^{0.1/2*0.0318}} \tag{1.19}$$
$$= 0.34v$$
$$V_3 = -1.65v$$
$$V_4 = -0.34v$$
$$\%Tilt = \frac{V_1 - V_2}{V_1} * 100$$
$$= \frac{1.65 - 0.34}{1.65} * 100$$
$$= 79.3\%$$

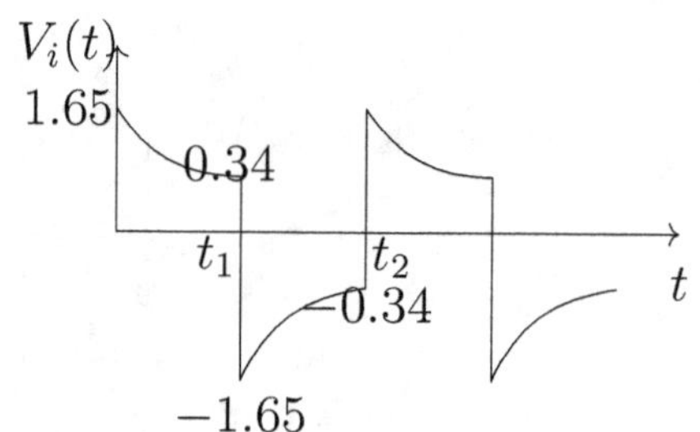

4. A square wave whose peak to peak value is 1 volt extends $\pm 0.5v$ with respect to ground. The duration of positive section is 0.1sec and negative section is 0.2sec. If this waveform is applied to a differentiating circuit whose time constant is 0.2sec. What are steady state maximum.

Solution:

Given: A=1V, T_1=0.1sec, T_2=0.2sec, RC=0.2sec

$$
\begin{aligned}
V_2 &= V_1 e^{-t_1/RC} \\
&= V_1 e^{-0.1/0.2} \\
&= 0.606 V_1 \\
V_3 &= V_2 - 1 \\
&= V_2 - A \\
V_4 &= V_3 e^{-t_2/RC} \\
&= V_3 e^{-0.2/0.2} \\
&= 0.367 V_3 \\
V_1 &= V_4 + A \\
&= V_4 + 1 \\
V_3 &= 0.606 V_1 - 1 \\
V_1 &= 0.367 V_3 + 1
\end{aligned}
\tag{1.20}
$$

Solving for V_1, V_2, V_3 and V_4

V_1 =0.81v and V_3=-0.5v

V_2 =0.5v and V_4=-0.19

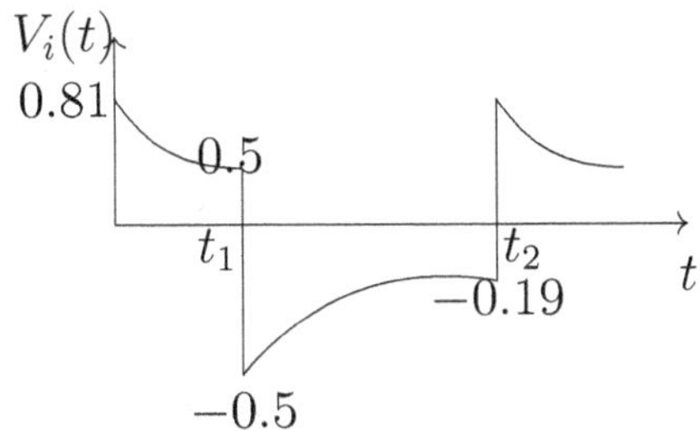

1.3.5   Sinusoidal Signal to High Pass RC

Applying Laplace transform to High Pass RC circuit.

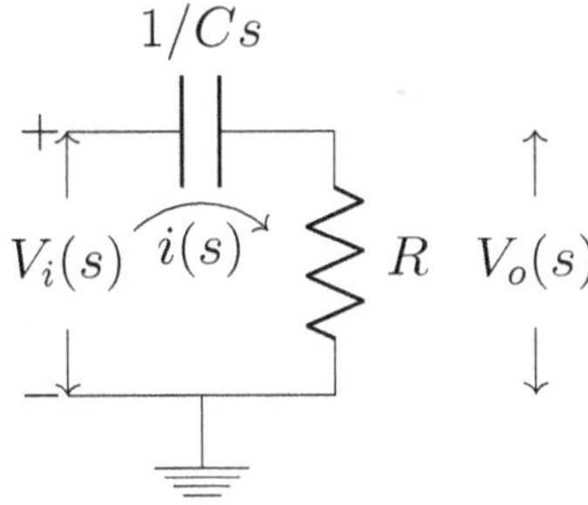

Finding the gain of the circuit,

$$\frac{V_0(s)}{V_i(s)} = \frac{RI(s)}{I(s)[R + 1/Cs]} \tag{1.21}$$
$$= \frac{RCs}{1 + RCs}$$

substituing s=jω

$$= \frac{j\omega RC}{1 + \omega RC} \tag{1.22}$$

Applying modulus on both sides, we get

$$= \frac{\omega RC}{\sqrt{1 + (\omega RC)^2}} \tag{1.23}$$

Bandwidth

It is defined as the range of frequencies for which gain does not fall below $1/\sqrt{(2)}$ or 3dB or 0.707. The upper 3dB frequency f_2 is ∞.

$$\frac{1}{\sqrt{2}} = \frac{2\pi f_1 RC}{\sqrt{1 + (2\pi f_1 RC)^2}}$$

$$f_1 = \frac{1}{2\pi RC} \tag{1.24}$$

where f_1 is Lower 3dB frequency

Bandwidth$= f_2 - f_1 = \infty$.

Problem:

1. A 10Hz square wave is fed to an amplifier. Calculate and plot output waveform for the following conditions. The lower 3dB frequency are 0.3Hz, 3Hz and 30Hz.

   Solution:

   Given: $f = 10$Hz.

   (a) $f_1 = 0.3$Hz

$$f_1 = \frac{1}{2\pi RC} = 0.3$$

$$RC = 0.53$$

$$V_1 = \frac{A}{1 + e^{-T/2RC}}$$

$$= \frac{A}{1 + e^{-0.1/2 \times 0.53}}$$

$$= 0.52 Av \tag{1.25}$$

$$V_2 = \frac{A}{1 + e^{T/2RC}}$$

$$= \frac{A}{1 + e^{0.1/2 \times 0.53}}$$

$$= 0.48 Av$$

$$V_3 = -0.52 Av$$

$$V_4 = -0.48 Av$$

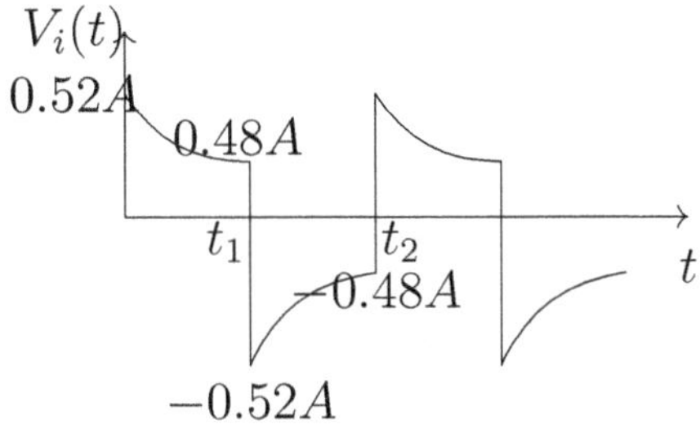

(b) f_2=3Hz

$$f_1 = \frac{1}{2\pi RC} = 3$$

$$RC = 0.05$$

$$V_1 = \frac{A}{1 + e^{-T/2RC}}$$
$$= \frac{A}{1 + e^{-0.1/2 \times 0.05}}$$
$$= 0.73Av \qquad (1.26)$$
$$V_2 = \frac{A}{1 + e^{T/2RC}}$$
$$= \frac{A}{1 + e^{0.1/2 \times 0.05}}$$
$$= 0.26Av$$
$$V_3 = -0.73Av$$
$$V_4 = -0.26Av$$

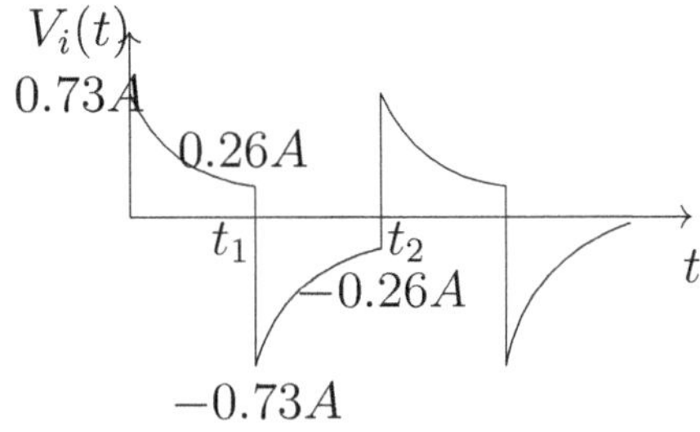

(c) f_2=30Hz

$$f_1 = \frac{1}{2\pi RC} = 30$$

$$RC = 0.005$$

$$V_1 = \frac{A}{1 + e^{-T/2RC}}$$
$$= \frac{A}{1 + e^{-0.1/2 \times 0.005}}$$
$$= 0.99Av \tag{1.27}$$

$$V_2 = \frac{A}{1 + e^{T/2RC}}$$
$$= \frac{A}{1 + e^{0.1/2 \times 0.005}}$$
$$= 0v$$

$$V_3 = -0.99Av$$

$$V_4 = 0v$$

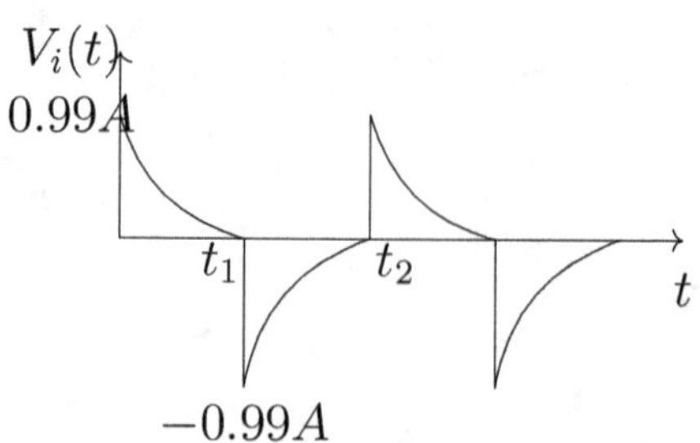

1.3.6 Relation between Lower 3dB frequency and %*tilt*:

$$\%t = \frac{T}{2RC} \times 100$$

$$f_1 = \frac{1}{2\pi RC}$$

$$RC = \frac{1}{2\pi f_1} \tag{1.28}$$

$$\%t = \frac{T}{2 \times \frac{1}{2\times\pi f_1}} \times 100$$

$$= \pi f_1 T \times 100$$

Problem:

1. A symmmetrical square wave $\pm 5v$ at a frequency of 5kHz is applied to high pass RC with cut off frequency of 20KHz. Sketch the input and ouput waveforms.

Solution:

Given A=10v, f=5KHz, f_1=20KHz

$$f_1 = \frac{1}{2\pi RC} = 20K$$

$$RC = 7.95\mu$$

$$V_1 = \frac{A}{1 + e^{-T/2RC}}$$

$$= \frac{A}{1 + e^{-0.2/2\times 7.95\mu}}$$

$$= 9.99v \tag{1.29}$$

$$V_2 = \frac{A}{1 + e^{T/2RC}}$$

$$= \frac{A}{1 + e^{0.2/2\times 7.95\mu}}$$

$$= 0.01v$$

$$V_3 = -9.99v$$

$$V_4 = -0.01v$$

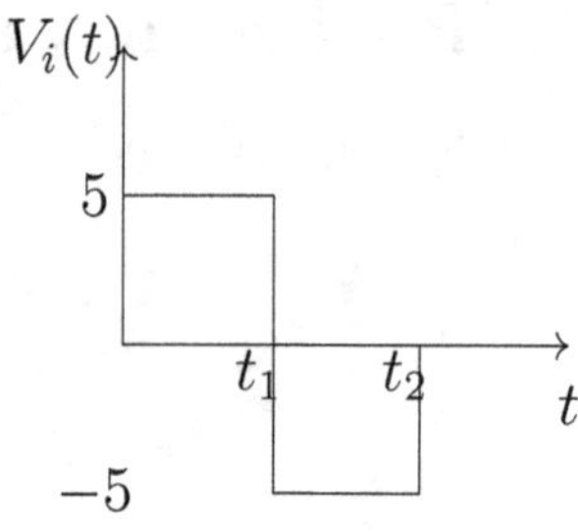

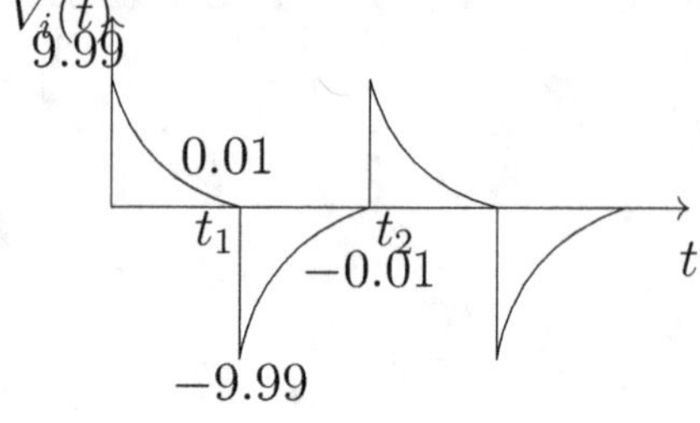

(a) Input Waveform   (b) Output Waveform

2. If a square wave of 5KHz is applied to high pass RC and resultant wave
   form is as shown in below figure. Find the lower 3dB frequency.

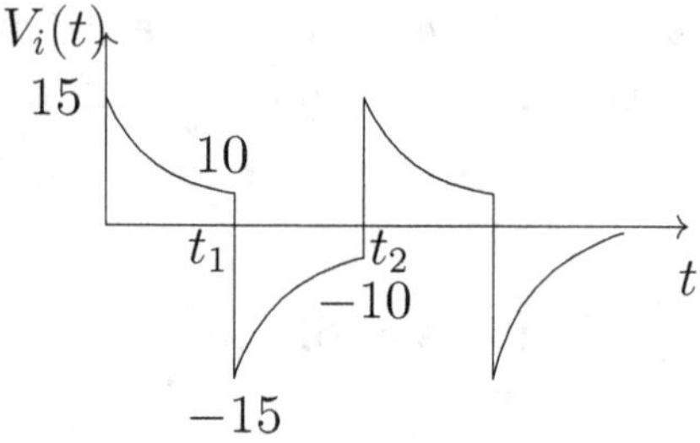

Solution:

Given f=5KHz, V_1=15, V_2=10

$$\%Tilt = \frac{V_1 - V_2}{V_1} \times 100$$

$$= \frac{15 - 10}{15} \times 100$$

$$= 33\% \tag{1.30}$$

$$\%t = \pi f_1 T \times 100$$

$$0.33 = \pi \times f_1 \times 0.2 \times 10^{-3} \times 100$$

$$f_1 = 525.2 Hz$$

3. A 10KHz square wave is applied to high pass RC produces the output
   with a tilt of 3.8%. Calculate lower 3dB frequency if the circuit uses a
   capacitor of 0.47μf also find resistance.

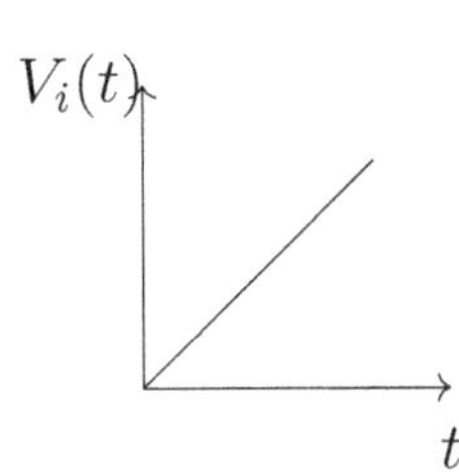

(a) Ramp Input

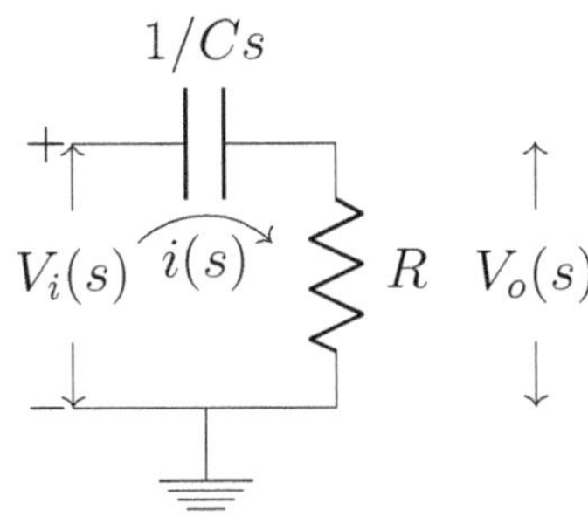

(b) Laplace Transofrm High Pass RC

Solution:

Given f=10KHz, %t=3.8, C=0.47 μf

$$
\begin{aligned}
\%t &= \frac{\pi f_1}{f} \times 100 \\
f_1 &= \frac{0.38 \times 10 \times 10^3}{\pi} \\
&= 120.95 Hz \\
f_1 &= \frac{1}{2\pi RC} \\
R &= 2.79 K\Omega
\end{aligned}
\tag{1.31}
$$

1.3.7   Ramp Input to High Pass RC

$$V_i(t) = \alpha t$$

$$V_i(s) = \frac{\alpha}{s^2}$$

$$\frac{V_0(s)}{V_i(s)} = \frac{RI(s)}{I(s)[R + 1/Cs]}$$

$$= \frac{RCs}{1 + RCs} \tag{1.32}$$

$$V_0(s) = V_i(s)[\frac{sRC}{sRC + 1}]$$

$$= \frac{\alpha}{s^2}[\frac{sRC}{sRC + 1}]$$

$$= \frac{\alpha}{s}[\frac{1}{s + 1/RC}]$$

Applying Partial Fractions

$$V_0(s) = \frac{\alpha}{s}[\frac{1}{s + 1/RC}] = \frac{a}{S} + \frac{b}{s + 1/RC}$$

$$\frac{\alpha}{s}[\frac{1}{s + 1/RC}] = \frac{a[s + 1/RC] + bs}{s[s + 1/RC]}$$

$$a[s + 1/RC] + bs = \alpha$$

$$as + a/RC + bs = \alpha$$

$$s(a + b) + a/RC = \alpha \tag{1.33}$$

$$a = -b, a = \alpha RC$$

$$V_0(s) = \frac{\alpha RC}{S} - \frac{\alpha RC}{s + 1/RC}$$

$$= \alpha RC[\frac{1}{s} - \frac{1}{s + 1/RC}]$$

Applying inverse laplace transfrom

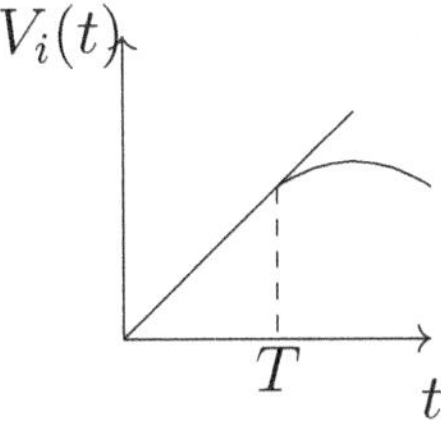

Figure 1.12: Output waveform of High Pass for Ramp Input

$$v_o(t) = \alpha RC[1 - e^{-t/RC}]$$

$$v_o(t) = \alpha RC[1 - (1 - \frac{t}{RC} + (\frac{t}{RC})^2 \times \frac{1}{2}] \tag{1.34}$$

$$\boxed{v_o(t) = \alpha t[1 - \frac{t}{2RC}]}$$

1.3.8 Transmission Error

It is defined as the time at which the output deviates from the input.

$$e_t = \frac{V_i(t) - V_o(t)}{V_i(t)}|t = T$$

$$= \frac{\alpha t - [\alpha t(1 - \frac{t}{2RC}]}{\alpha t}|t = T \tag{1.35}$$

$$\boxed{e_t = \frac{T}{2RC}}$$

1.3.9 Relation between Lower 3dB frequency and Transmission error

$$e_t = \frac{T}{2RC}$$

$$f_1 = \frac{1}{2\pi RC} \tag{1.36}$$

$$\boxed{e_t = \pi f_1 T}$$

Problems:

1. A limited ramp as shown in figure is applied to a differentiator. Draw the output for

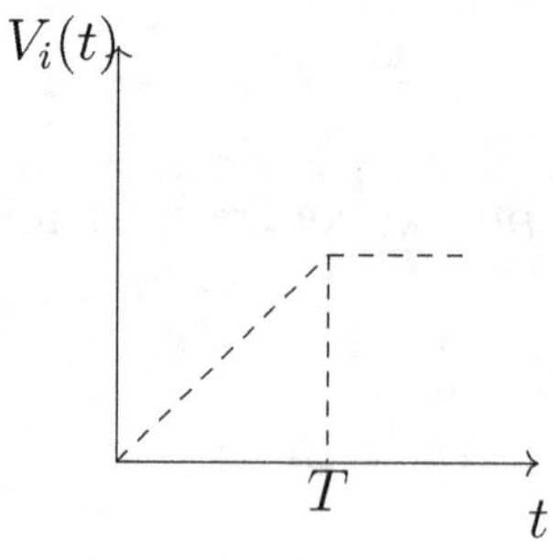

(a) T=0.2RC

(b) T=2RC

(c) T=5RC

Solution:

(a)

$$v_o(t) = \alpha RC\left[1 - e^{\frac{t}{2RC}}\right]$$

$$\alpha = \frac{V_i(t)}{T}$$

$$RC = 5T \tag{1.37}$$

$$v_o(t) = \frac{V_i(t)}{T} \times 5T \times \left[1 - e^{\frac{T}{5T}}\right]$$

$$= 0.906V_i$$

(b)

$$v_o(t) = \alpha RC\left[1 - e^{\frac{t}{2RC}}\right]$$

$$\alpha = \frac{V_i(t)}{T}$$

$$RC = 0.5T \tag{1.38}$$

$$v_o(t) = \frac{V_i(t)}{T} \times 0.5T \times \left[1 - e^{\frac{T}{0.5T}}\right]$$

$$= 0.432V_i$$

(c)

$$v_o(t) = \alpha RC[1 - e^{\frac{t}{2RC}}]$$

$$\alpha = \frac{V_i(t)}{T}$$

$$RC = 0.2T \tag{1.39}$$

$$v_o(t) = \frac{V_i(t)}{T} \times 0.2T \times [1 - e^{\frac{T}{0.2T}}]$$

$$= 0.19V_i$$

2. For high pass filter it is desired to pass 3ms sweep for ramp input with not less than 0.5% transmission error. Determine the highest possible value of lower 3dB frequency.

Solution:

Given: T=3ms, e_t=0.5%

$$e_t = \pi f_1 T$$

$$f_1 = \frac{e_t}{\pi T}$$

$$= \frac{0.005}{\pi \times 3 \times 10^{-3}} \tag{1.40}$$

$$= 0.53 Hz$$

Statement:

For any periodic input waveform under steady state conditions, the average value of the output waveform for high pass RC circuit is equal to zero.

Proof:

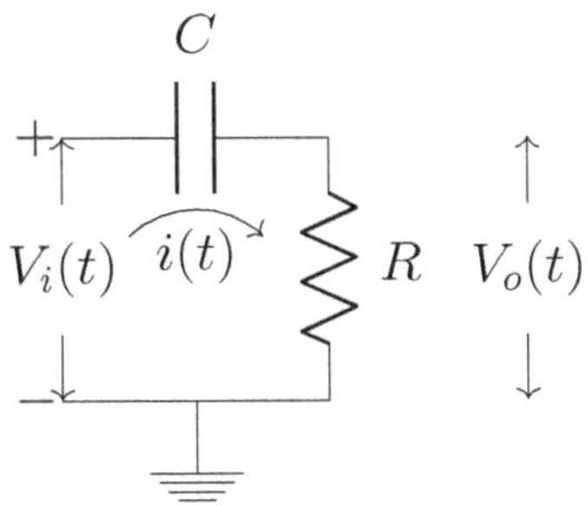

$$\begin{aligned}
V_i(t) &= V_C + V_R \\
&= V_C + V_o(t) \\
&= \frac{q}{C} + V_o(t)
\end{aligned} \tag{1.41}$$

where q is the charge of the capacitance

Differentiating the circuit wrt to t

$$\begin{aligned}
\frac{dV_i(t)}{dt} &= \frac{1}{C}\frac{dq}{dt} + V_o(t) \\
\frac{dV_i(t)}{dt} &= \frac{i}{C} + V_o(t)
\end{aligned} \tag{1.42}$$

multiplying dt on both sides

$$dV_i(t) = \frac{i}{C}idt + dV_o(t) \tag{1.43}$$

Applying intergration on both sides

$$\int_0^T dV_i(t) = \frac{1}{C}\int_0^T idt + \int_0^T dV_o(t)$$

$$V_i(t)|_0^T = \frac{1}{RC}\int_0^T V_o(t)dt + V_o(t)|_0^T \tag{1.44}$$

$$\boxed{\frac{1}{RC}\int_0^T V_o(t)dt = 0}$$

1.3.10   High Pass RC as Differentiator

Condition: At very very small time constant, high pass RC circuit will act as a Differentiator.

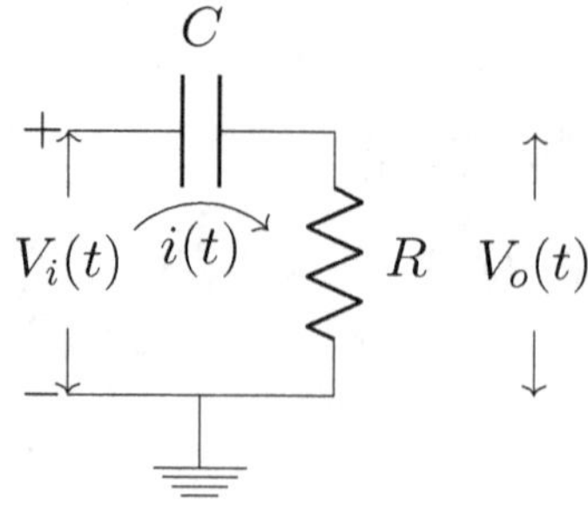

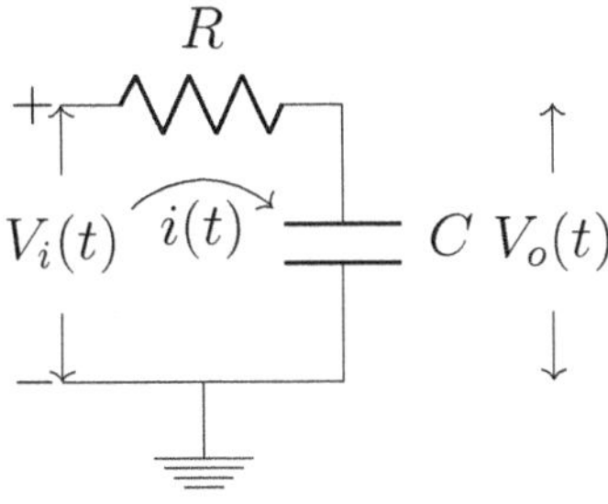

Figure 1.13: Low Pass RC circuit

neglecting the voltage across the resistor

$$i = C\frac{\mathrm{d}V_c(t)}{\mathrm{d}t}$$
$$i = C\frac{\mathrm{d}V_i(t)}{\mathrm{d}t} \tag{1.45}$$
$$V_o(t) = iR$$

$$\boxed{V_o(t) = RC\frac{\mathrm{d}V_i(t)}{\mathrm{d}t}}$$

1.4 Low Pass RC circuit

1.4.1 Step Input to Low Pass RC

When a step input is applied to High Pass RC as shown in figure 1.13, capacitor does not charge instantaneously. So, V_i=0.

As time increases, capacitor starts charging and it can charge upto the maximum input volage i.e A. So, V_f=A.

$$V_o(t) = V_f + (V_i - V_f)e^{-t/RC} \tag{1.46}$$
$$V_o(t) = A + (0 - A)e^{-t/RC}$$
$$= A[1 - [e^{-t/RC}]] \tag{1.47}$$

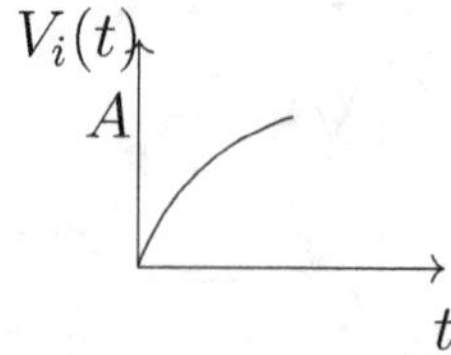

Figure 1.14: Output Waveform of Low Pass for Step Input signal

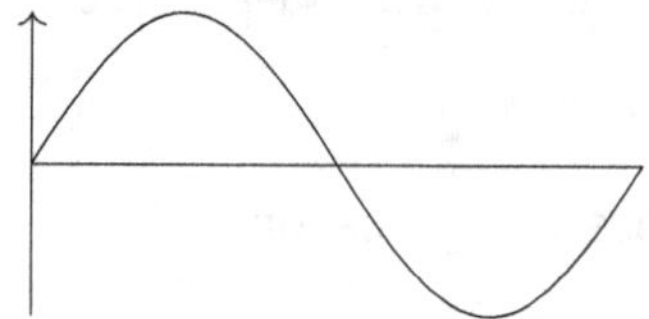

Figure 1.15: Sinusoidal Signal

1.4.2 Sinusoidal Signal to Low Pass RC circuit

When a figure 1.15 is applied to Low pass RC circuit as shown in the figure 1.13. If the frequency is zero, reactance of the capacitance is ∞, then $V_o(t)=V_i(t)$ and If the frequency is ∞, reactance of the capacitance is zero, the $V_o(t)=0$.

Applying Laplace Transofrm to the circuit shown in the figure 1.13

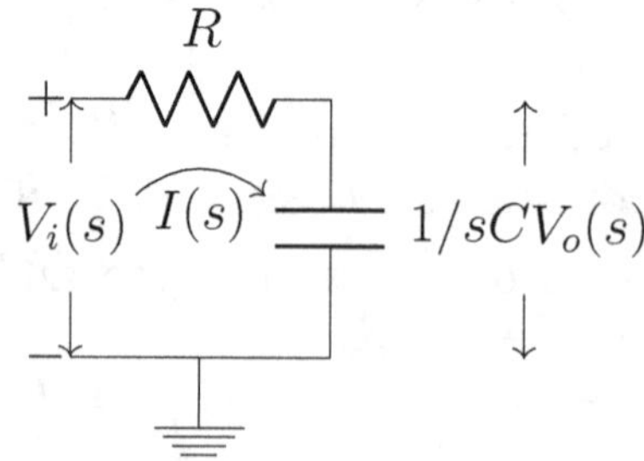

Figure 1.16: Laplace Transform representation of Low Pass RC circuit

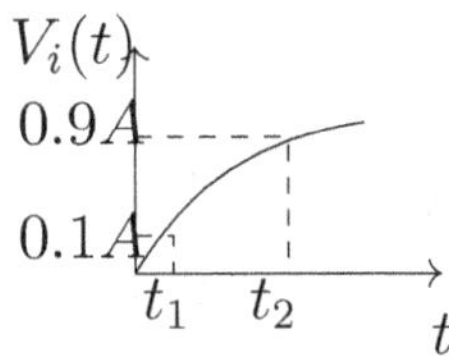

Figure 1.17: Waveform to caluclate Rise Time

$$\frac{V_o(s)}{V_i(s)} = \frac{I(s)\frac{1}{sC}}{I(s)[R + \frac{1}{sC}]}$$
$$= \frac{1}{1 + sRC} \tag{1.48}$$

Replacing s=j ω

$$\frac{V_o(s)}{V_i(s)} = \frac{1}{1 + j\omega RC} \tag{1.49}$$

Applying modulos on both sides and simplying the equation to find the upper 3dB frequency

$$\frac{1}{\sqrt{2}} = \frac{1}{\sqrt{1 + (\omega RC)^2}} \tag{1.50}$$

$$\boxed{f_2 = \frac{1}{2\pi RC}}$$

where f_2 is the upper 3dB frequency.

Band width of Low Pass RC circuit is given as $f_2\text{-}f_1 = f_2$

1.4.3 Rise Time

It is defined as time taken by the output waveform for a step input signal to reach from 10% of final output voltage to 90% of final output voltage. From the waveform shown in the figure 1.17, rise time t_r is calculated using the ouput equaiton of step input to Low Pass RC circuit as

$$V_o(t) = A[1 - [e^{-t/RC}]]$$

$$0.1A = A[1 - [e^{-t_1/RC}]]$$

$$e^{-t_1/RC} = 0.9$$

$$-t_1/RC = ln(0.9)$$

$$\boxed{t_1 = 0.1RC}$$

$$0.9A = A[1 - [e^{-t_2/RC}]] \tag{1.51}$$

$$e^{-t_1/RC} = 0.1$$

$$-t_1/RC = ln(0.1)$$

$$\boxed{t_1 = 2.3RC}$$

$$t_r = t_2 - t_1$$

$$\boxed{t_r = 2.2RC}$$

1.4.4   Relation between Rise Time and Upper 3dB frequency

The relation is given as

$$\boxed{t_r = 2.2RC}$$

$$\boxed{f_2 = \frac{1}{2\pi RC}}$$

$$RC = \frac{1}{2\pi f_2} \tag{1.52}$$

$$t_r = 2.2 \times \frac{1}{2\pi f_2}$$

$$\boxed{t_r = \frac{0.35}{f_2}}$$

Probelm: A step input of 10v is applied to Low Pass RC with a rise time of 200 μ f. Calculate Upper 3dB frequency. If the capacitance is 0.47 μ f, find Resistance.

 Solution: Given V=10, t_r=20 μf, C= 0.47 μf

 Substituting the given values in Rise Time formulae

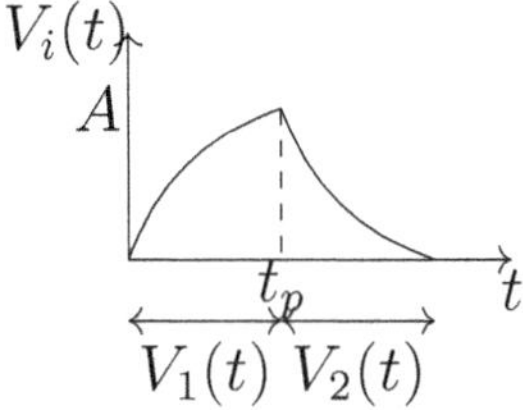

Figure 1.18: Output Waveform of Low Pass for Pulse Input signal

$$t_r = \frac{0.35}{f_2}$$

$$200 \times 10^{-6} = \frac{0.35}{f_2} \tag{1.53}$$

$$\boxed{f_2 = 1750Hz}$$

Substituing Upper 3dB frequency, we get

$$f_2 = \frac{1}{2\pi RC}$$

$$1750 = \frac{1}{2\pi \times 0.47 \times 10^{-6}} \tag{1.54}$$

$$\boxed{R = 193.5\Omega}$$

1.4.5 Pulse Input to Low Pass RC Circuit

If the figure shown in 1.2 is applied to the Low Pass RC circuit shown in 1.13, the output is shown in the figure 1.18 Caluclating $V_1(t)$ and $V_2(t)$

$$V_1(t) = A[1 - [e^{-t/RC}]] \tag{1.55}$$

at t=t_p, $V_1(t)$=$V_p(t)$

$$\boxed{V_p(t) = A[1 - [e^{-t_p/RC}]]} \tag{1.56}$$

$$V_2(t) = V_f + (V_i - V_f)e^{-(t-t_p)/RC}$$

substituing $V_f =0$, $V_i=V_p$

$$V_2(t) = 0 + (V_p - 0)e^{-(t-t_p)/RC}$$

$$\boxed{V_2(t) = V_p e^{-(t-t_p)/RC}} \tag{1.57}$$

$$V_o(t) = V_1(t) + V_2(t)$$

Probelm

1. Determine the Upper 3dB frequency for Low Pass RC circuit if a pulse of 0.5μsec is required to pass without distortion. Find the value of Resistance if capacitance is 0.001μf.

Sloution:

Given $t_p=0.5\mu$sec, C=0.001μf. The Upper 3dB frequency is given as

$$f_2 = \frac{1}{t_p}$$

$$= \frac{1}{0.5 \times 10^{-6}} \tag{1.58}$$

$$\boxed{f_2 = 2MHz}$$

Substituing f_2 in Uppder 3dB frqeuncy to calculate Resistance

$$f_2 = \frac{1}{2\pi RC}$$

$$R = \frac{1}{2\pi \times 0.001 \times 10^{-6} \times 2 \times 10^6} \tag{1.59}$$

$$\boxed{R = 79.57\Omega}$$

2. An ideal 1μsec pulse is applied to an amplifier. Calculate and plot the output waveform for the following conditions. The upper 3dB frequency are 10MHz, 1MHz and 0.1MHz.

Solution

If the pulse input shown in the figure 1.2 is applied to Low Pass RC as shown in the figure 1.13, the output waveform for all 3 conditions is shown in the figure 1.19

(a) f_2=10MHz

$$f_2 = \frac{1}{2\pi RC}$$
$$RC = \frac{1}{2\pi f_2}$$
$$= \frac{1}{2\pi \times 10 \times 10^6} \tag{1.60}$$
$$= 1.59 \times 10^{-8} sec$$
$$V_p(t) = A[1 - [e^{-t_p/RC}]]$$
$$= A[1 - [e^{-1\times 10^{-6}/1.59\times 10^{-8}}]]$$
$$= Av$$

(b) f_2=1MHz

$$f_2 = \frac{1}{2\pi RC}$$
$$RC = \frac{1}{2\pi f_2}$$
$$= \frac{1}{2\pi \times 10^6} \tag{1.61}$$
$$= 1.59 \times 10^{-7} sec$$
$$V_p(t) = A[1 - [e^{-t_p/RC}]]$$
$$= A[1 - [e^{-1\times 10^{-6}/1.59\times 10^{-7}}]]$$
$$= 0.998Av$$

(c) f_2=0.1MHz

$$f_2 = \frac{1}{2\pi RC}$$
$$RC = \frac{1}{2\pi f_2}$$
$$= \frac{1}{2\pi \times 0.1 \times 10^6} \tag{1.62}$$
$$= 1.59 \times 10^{-6} sec$$
$$V_p(t) = A[1 - [e^{-t_p/RC}]]$$
$$= A[1 - [e^{-1\times 10^{-6}/1.59\times 10^{-6}}]]$$
$$= 0.466Av$$

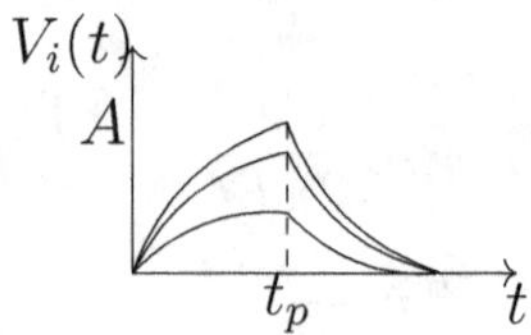

Figure 1.19: Output waveform

1.4.6   Square Wave to Low Pass RC Circuit

Assuming a symmetrical square wave shown in the figure 1.3 is applied to Low Pass RC Circuit shown in the figure 1.13, where $A_2=|A_1|=\frac{A}{2}$, $T_1=T_2$. Using the generalized equation,

$$V_o(t) = V_f + (V_i - V_f)e^{-t/RC}$$

$$V_01(t) = V_f + (V_i - V_f)e^{-T_1/RC} \tag{1.63}$$

where $V_f=A_1$, $V_i=V_1$

$$V_01(t) = A_1 + (V_1 - A_1)e^{-T/2RC}$$

$$V_2 = \frac{A}{2} + (-V_2 - \frac{A}{2})e^{-T/2RC}$$

$$V_2[1 + e^{-T/2RC}] = \frac{A}{2} + [1 - e^{-T/2RC}] \tag{1.64}$$

$$V_2 = \frac{A}{2}[\frac{1 - e^{-T/2RC}}{1 + e^{-T/2RC}}]$$

$$= \frac{A}{2}[\frac{e^{T/2RC} - 1}{e^{T/2RC} + 1}]$$

Assuming T/2RC=2x

$$V_2 = \frac{A}{2}[\frac{e^{2x} - 1}{e^{2x} + 1}]$$

$$= \frac{A}{2}[\frac{e^x - e^{-x}}{e^x + e^{-x}}]$$

$$= \frac{A}{2}[\frac{\sinh x}{\cosh x}] \tag{1.65}$$

$$\boxed{V_2 = \frac{A}{2}\tanh x}$$

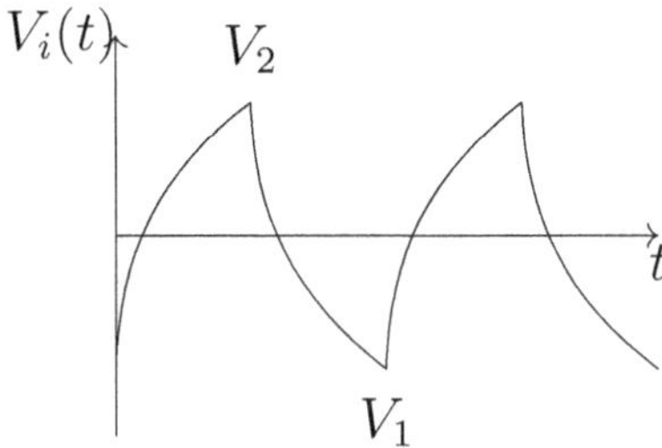

Figure 1.20: Output Waveform of Low Pass for Square signal

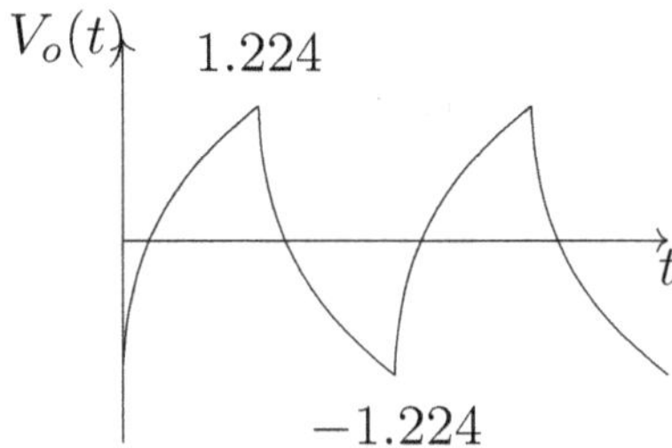

Figure 1.21: Output Waveform

Problems

1. A symmetrical square wave of amplitude $\pm 5v$ and frequency of 2KHz is applied to Low Pass RC. If R=5KΩ, C=0.1μf, calculate and plot the output. **Solution:**

   Given: A=10v, R=5KΩ, C=0.1μf, f=2KHz. Substituing in the formulae of V_2,

$$V_2 = \frac{A}{2}[\frac{1 - e^{-T/2RC}}{1 + e^{-T/2RC}}]$$
$$= \frac{10}{2}[\frac{1 - e^{-0.5 \times 10^{-3}/2 \times 5 \times 10^3 \times 0.1 \times 10^{-6}}}{1 + e^{-0.5 \times 10^{-3}/2 \times 5 \times 10^3 \times 0.1 \times 10^{-6}}}]$$
$$= 5[\frac{1 - 0.606}{1 + 0.606}] \tag{1.66}$$

$$\boxed{V_2 = 1.224v}$$
$$\boxed{V_1 = -1.224v}$$

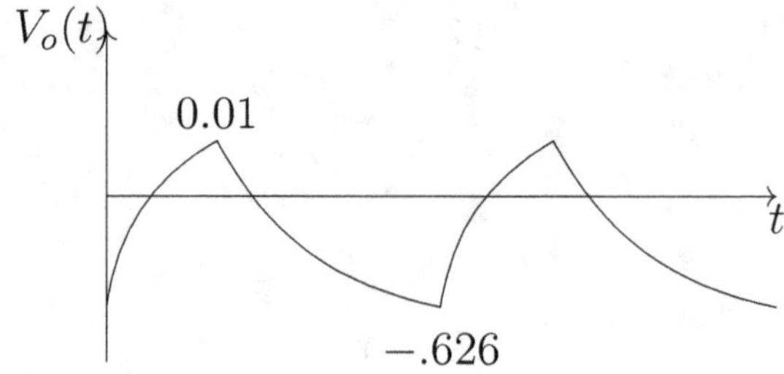

Figure 1.22: Output Waveform

2. A square wave whose peak to peak amplitude is 2v extends $\pm 1v$. The duration of positive section is 0.1sec and that of negative section is 0.2sec. If this waveforem is applied to RC intergrating circuit whose time constant is 0.2sec. What are steady state maximum and minimum values. **Solution:**

Given: Square wave is asymmetrical, A=2v, T_1=0.1sec, T_1=0.2sec, RC=0.2, V_f=1. Substituing in the generalized equation. The ouput waveform is shown in the figure 1.22

$$V_o(t) = V_f + (V_i - V_f)e^{-t/RC}$$
$$V_0 1(t) = 1 + (V_1 - 1)e^{-0.1/0.2}$$
$$V_2 = 1 + (V_1 - 1)e^{-0.1/0.2} \tag{1.67}$$
$$V_0 2(t) = -1 + (V_2 + 1)e^{-0.2/0.2}$$
$$V_1 = -1 + (V_2 + 1)e^{-1}$$

solving for V_1 and V_2

$$\boxed{V_1 = -0.626v}$$
$$\boxed{V_2 = 0.01v} \tag{1.68}$$

1.4.7   Ramp Signal to Low Pass RC circuit

Ramp signal shown in the figure 1.4 is applied to Low Pass RC Circuit shown in the figure 1.13. The output waveform i shown in the figure 1.23

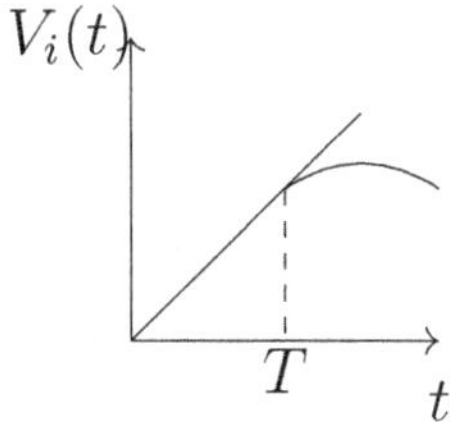

Figure 1.23: Output waveform of Low Pass for Ramp Input

$$V_i = V_R + V_C$$
$$= V_R + V_o(t)$$
$$V_o(t) = V_i - V_R \tag{1.69}$$

$$\boxed{V_o(t) = \alpha t - \alpha RC(1 - e^{-t/RC})}$$

where $V_R = V_o(t)$ for Ramp Input signal to High Pass RC Circuit

1.4.8 Transmission Error

$$e_t = \frac{V_i(t) - V_o(t)}{V_i(t)} \mid t = T$$
$$= \frac{\alpha t - \alpha t + \alpha RC(1 - e^{-t/RC})}{\alpha t} \mid t = T \tag{1.70}$$

$$\boxed{e_t = \frac{RC}{T}(1 - e^{-t/RC})}$$

$$\boxed{e_t = \frac{RC}{T}}$$

Problem For a Low Pass RC filter it is desired to pass a 3msec sweep for a Ramp input less than 0.5% transmission error. Determine maximum possible value of Upper 3dB frequency.

Solution:

Given: $e_t = 0.5\%$, T=3msec. Substituting in transmission error

$$e_t = \frac{RC}{T}$$

$$Rc = e_t \times T$$

$$= 0.005 \times 3 \times 10^{-3}$$

$$\boxed{RC = 0.015 msec}$$

(1.71)

$$f_2 = \frac{1}{2\pi RC}$$

$$= \frac{1}{2\pi \times 0.015 \times 10^{-3}}$$

$$\boxed{f_2 = 10.6 KHz}$$

1.4.9   Low Pass RC Circuit as Integrator

Condition: At very very large time constant, Low pass RC circuit will act as a Intergrator.

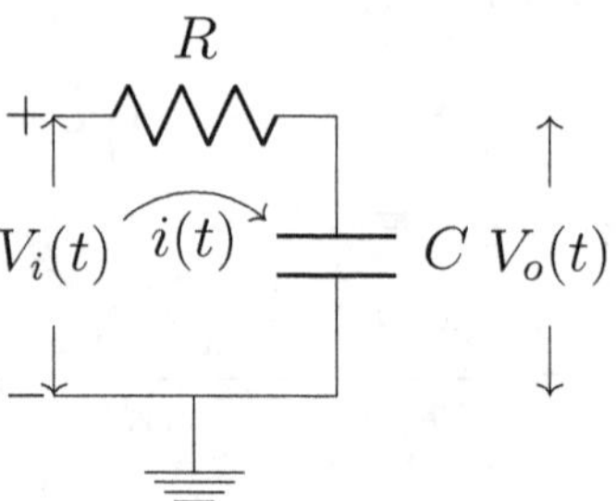

From the circuit,

$$V_i = V_R + V_C$$

(1.72)

since capacitor neither charges or discharges instantaneously

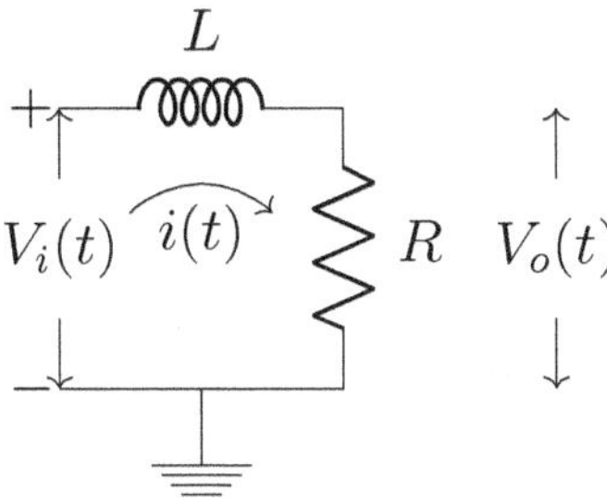

Figure 1.24: Low Pass RL Circuit

$$V_i \approx V_R$$

$$V_o(t) = \frac{1}{C} \int_0^T i \, dt$$

$$= \frac{1}{C} \int_0^T \frac{V_i(t)}{R} \, dt \qquad (1.73)$$

$$\boxed{V_o(t) = \frac{1}{RC} \int_0^T V_i(t) \, dt}$$

1.5 RL Circuits

The capacitor C in RC circuits is replaced with an inductor L to design RL circuits. The time constant of RL circuit is $\frac{L}{R}$.

1.5.1 Low Pass RL Circuit

The circuit of Low Pass RL is shown in 1.24. The reactance of the inductance is given as $X_L = 2\pi f L$. At very low frequencies the reactance offered by the inductor is very small. Due to this,the output across the resistor is equal to the input (f=0, T=∞, X_L=0, $V_o(t)$=$V_i(t)$). As the frequency increases, the reactance offered by the inductor increases such that the signal gets attenuated. So the output is almost equal to zero (f=∞, T=0, X_L=∞, $V_o(t)$=0). So the circuit acts as Low Pass Filter.

(a)   (b)

Figure 1.25: (a) Step Input (b) Output of Low Pass RL Circuit

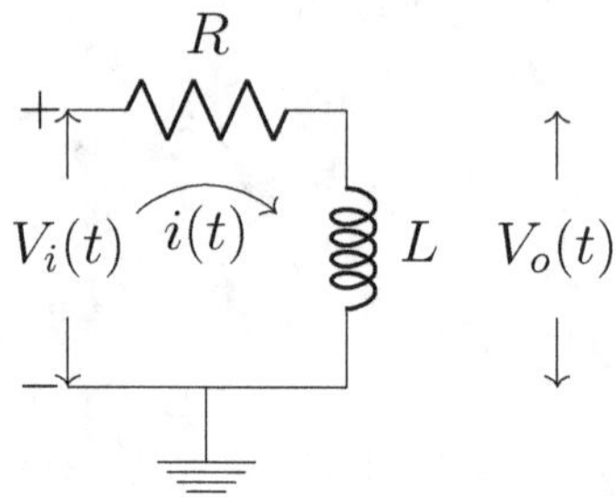

Figure 1.26: High Pass RL Circuit

Step Input to Low Pass RL Circuit

Using the generalized output expression
$$V_o(t) = V_f + (V_i - V_f)e^{-Rt/L} \qquad (1.74)$$
When a step input signal is fed a to Low Pass RL Circuit as shown in figure 1.24, Intially, reactance of the inductor is zero. So, V_i=0.

As time increases, reactance of the indcutor increases and it can reach upto the maximum input volage i.e A. So, V_f=A. The input and output waveform is shown in the figure 1.25.
$$V_o(t) = A + (0 - A)e^{-Rt/L}$$
$$\boxed{V_o(t) = A[1 + e^{-Rt/L}]} \qquad (1.75)$$

1.5.2 High Pass RL Circuit

The circuit of High Pass RL is shown in 1.26. The reactance of the inductance

Figure 1.27: (a) Step Input (b) Output of High Pass RL Circuit

is given as $X_L=2\pi fL$. At very low frequencies the reactance offered by the inductor is small. Due to this,the output across the inductor is equal to zero (f=0, T=∞, X_L=0, $V_o(t)$=0). As the frequency increases, the reactance offered by the inductor increases. At such high frequencies the output is equal to input (f=∞, T=0, X_L=∞, $V_o(t)$=$V_i(t)$). So the circuit acts as High Pass Filter.

Step Input to High Pass RL Circuit

Using the generalized output expression
$$V_o(t) = V_f + (V_i - V_f)e^{-Rt/L} \tag{1.76}$$
When a step input signal is fed a to Low Pass RL Circuit as shown in figure 1.26, Intially, reactance of inductor is zero. So, V_i=A.

As time increases, reactance of the inductor increases and it can reach upto the maximum input volage i.e A. So, V_f=0. The input and output waveform is shown in the figure 1.27.
$$V_o(t) = 0 + (A - 0)e^{-Rt/L}$$
$$\boxed{V_o(t) = Ae^{-Rt/L}} \tag{1.77}$$

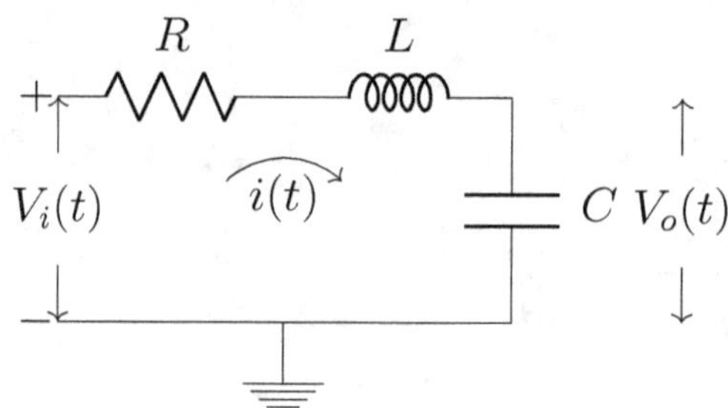

Figure 1.28: RLC Series Circuit

1.6   RLC Series Circuit

The figure 1.28 shows the RLC Series Circuit. Applying Laplace Transfrom
to the circuit,

$$\frac{V_o(s)}{V_i(s)} = \frac{I(s)[\frac{1}{sC}]}{I(s)[R + sL + \frac{1}{sC}]}$$

$$= \frac{1}{s^2 LC + sRC + 1} \tag{1.78}$$

$$\frac{V_o(s)}{V_i(s)} = \frac{1}{LC[s^2 + \frac{R}{L}s + \frac{1}{LC}]}$$

The roots of the characteristic equation s_1, s_2 are

$$s^2 + \frac{R}{L}s + \frac{1}{LC} = 0$$

$$s_1, s_2 = \frac{-R}{2L} \pm \sqrt{(\frac{R}{2L})^2 - \frac{1}{LC}} \tag{1.79}$$

- If $(\frac{R}{2L})^2 > \frac{1}{LC}$ the roots are real and different and the circuit is over-
  damped.

- If $(\frac{R}{2L})^2 = \frac{1}{LC}$ the roots are real and equal and the circuit iscritically
  damped.

- If $(\frac{R}{2L})^2 < \frac{1}{LC}$ the roots are complex and the circuit is underdamped.

The term $\sqrt{L/C}$ is known as the Charactersitic Impedance.

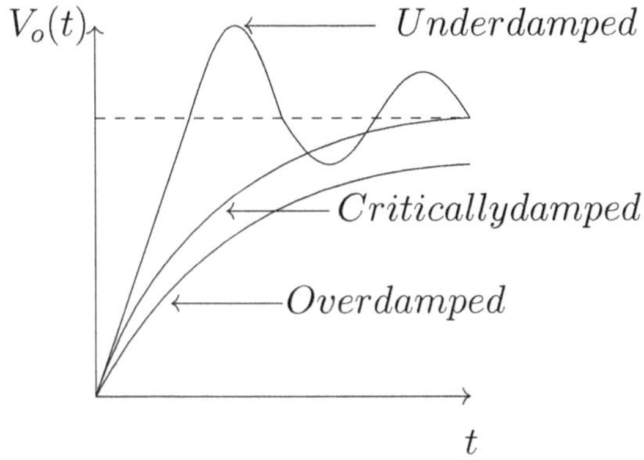

Figure 1.29: Response to step input signal

Step Input to RLC Circuit The response is shown in the figure 1.29. The input signal and output response is given as

$$V_i(s) = \frac{A}{s}$$

$$V_o(s) = (\frac{A}{LC})[\frac{1}{s[s^2 + \frac{R}{L}s + \frac{1}{LC}]}] \qquad (1.80)$$

A ***Ringing Circuit*** provides nearly undamped oscillations.

Chapter 2

Non Linear Wave Shaping

The process by which the shape of sinusoidal signal is changed by passing through a network which consists of non-linear elements is called Non-Linear wave shaping.There are two types of Non-Linear Wave Shaping circuits:

1. Clippers

2. Clampers

2.1   Clippers

It is a circuit which removes the un-wanted portion of the input signal. Diode is the main component in designing Clipper circuit. Based on the position of the diode, Clippers are classified into two types:

1. Series Clippers

2. Shunt Clippers

Based on the shape of output

1. Positive Clipper - Biased and Un-biased

2. Negative Clipper - Biased and Un-biased

3. Two Level Clipper

Since Diode is important component, conditions of forward and reverse bias are: Diode will be forward bias if the voltage at anode terminal is more than the voltage at cathode terminal otherwise diode gets reverse bias.

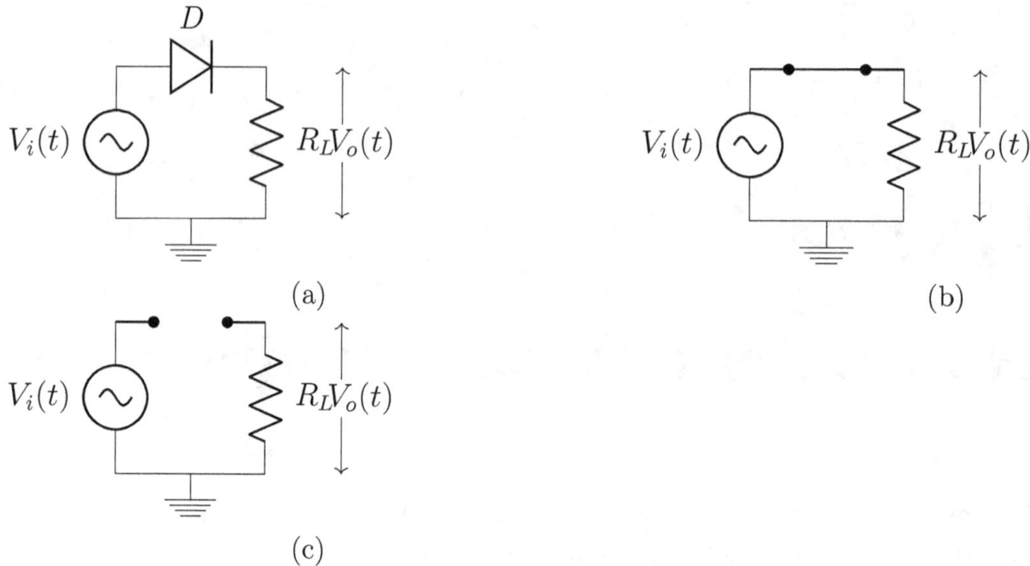

Figure 2.1: Ideal diode:(a) Circuit diagram (b) when diode is forward biased (c) when diode is reverse biased

2.1.1   Un-biased Series Negative Clipper

The circuit of Un-biased Series Negative Clipper is shown in the figure 2.1

Assuming Diode is Ideal

If $V_i(t)$<0, the diode is reverse biased and it acts as open circuit. The equivalent circuit is shown in 2.1. Then the output $V_o(t)$=0.

If $V_i(t)$>0, the diode is forward biased and it acts as short circuit. The equivalent circuit is shown in 2.1. Then the output $V_o(t)=V_i(t)$. The output wave form and transfer characteristics is shown in the figure 2.2.

Assuming Diode is Practical

If $V_i(t) < V_\gamma$, the diode is reverse biased and it acts as open circuit. The equivalent circuit is shown in 2.3. Then the output $V_o(t)$=0.

If $V_i(t) > V_\gamma$, the diode is forward biased and it is replaced with 0.7v battery. The equivalent circuit is shown in 2.3. Then the output $V_o(t)=V_i(t)$-V_γ. V_γ for silicon is 0.6 or 0.7v. The output wave form and transfer characteristics is shown in the figure 2.4.

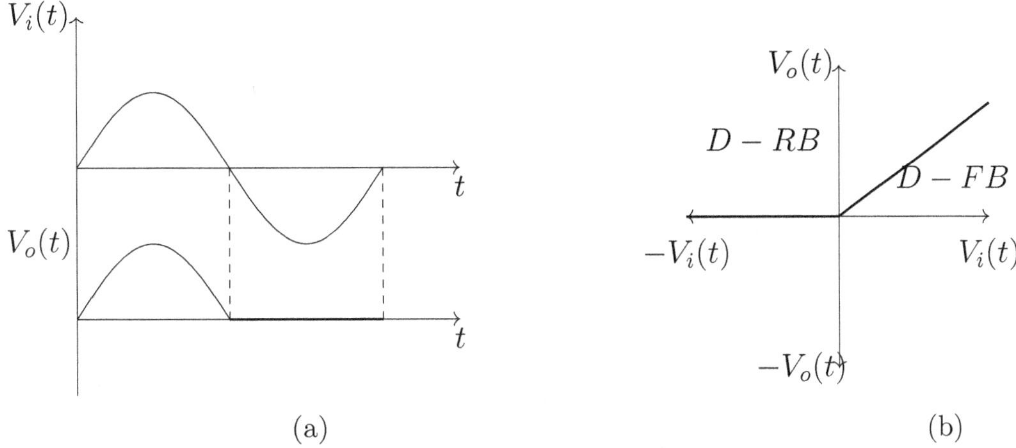

Figure 2.2: Ideal diode:(a) Input and Output waveform (b) Transfer Charactersitics

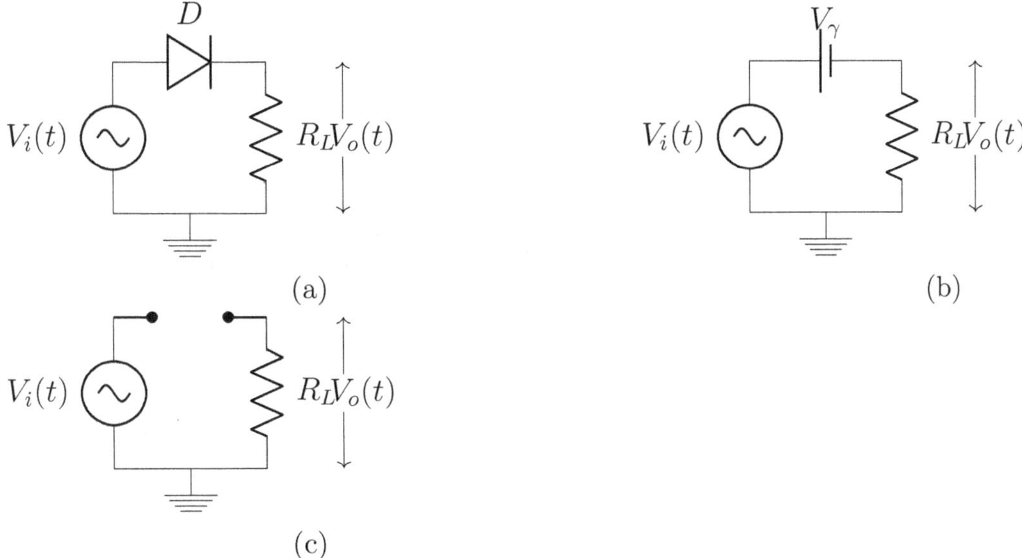

Figure 2.3: Practical diode:(a) Circuit diagram (b) when diode is forward biased (c) when diode is reverse biased

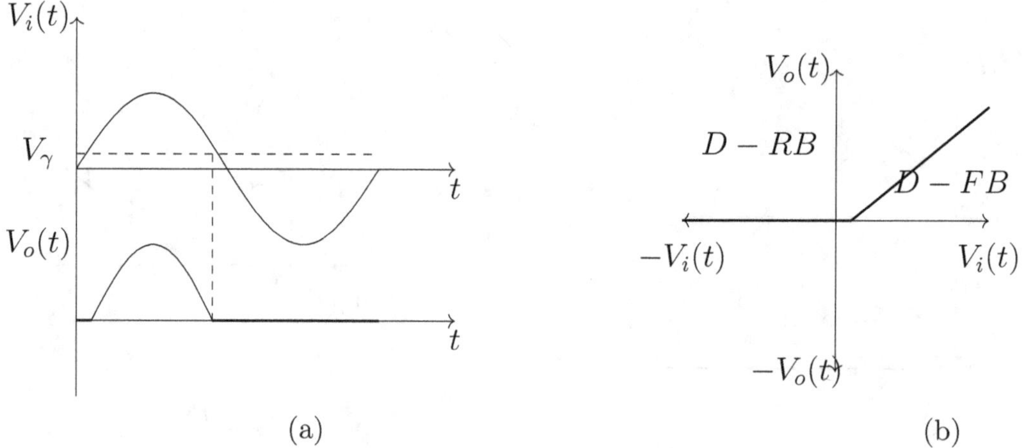

Figure 2.4: Practical diode:(a) Input and Output waveform (b) Transfer Charactersitics

2.1.2 Un-biased Series Positive Clipper

The circuit of Un-biased Series Positive Clipper is shown in the figure 2.5

Assuming Diode is Ideal

If $V_i(t)$<0, the diode is forward biased and it acts as short circuit. The equivalent circuit is shown in 2.5. Then the output $V_o(t)=V_i(t)$.

If $V_i(t)$>0, the diode is reverse biased and it acts as open circuit. The equivalent circuit is shown in 2.5. Then the output $V_o(t)=0$. The output wave form and transfer charactersitics is shown in the figure 2.6.

Assuming Diode is Practical

If $V_i(t) < V_\gamma$, the diode is forward biased and it acts as battery. The equivalent circuit is shown in 2.7. Then the output $V_o(t)=V_i(t)+V_\gamma$.

If $V_i(t) > V_\gamma$, the diode is reverse biased and it is replaced with open circuit. The equivalent circuit is shown in 2.7. Then the output $V_o(t)=0$. The output wave form and transfer charactersitics is shown in the figure 2.8.

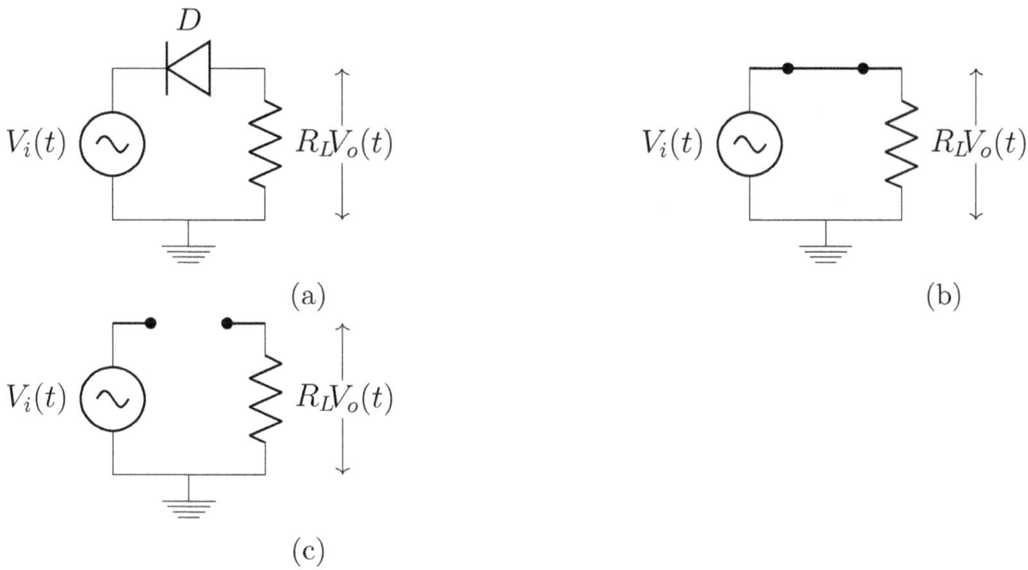

Figure 2.5: Ideal diode:(a) Circuit diagram (b) when diode is forward biased (c) when diode is reverse biased

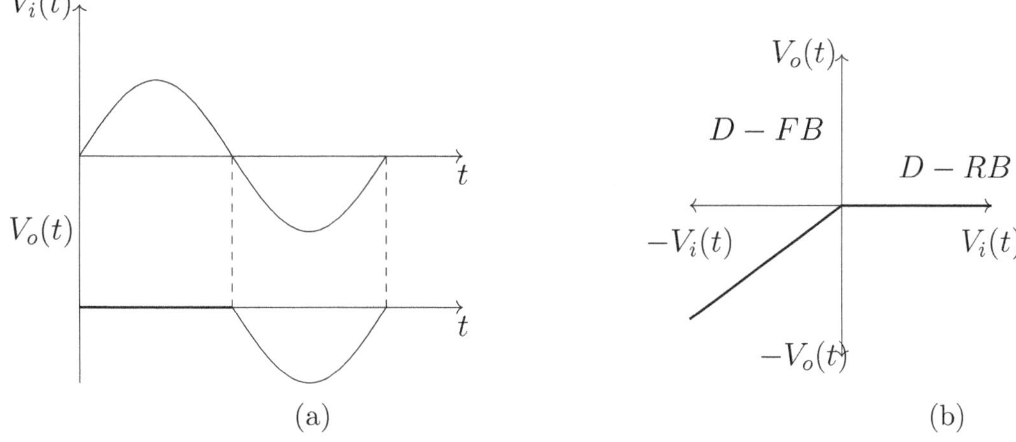

Figure 2.6: Ideal diode:(a) Input and Output waveform (b) Transfer Charactersitics

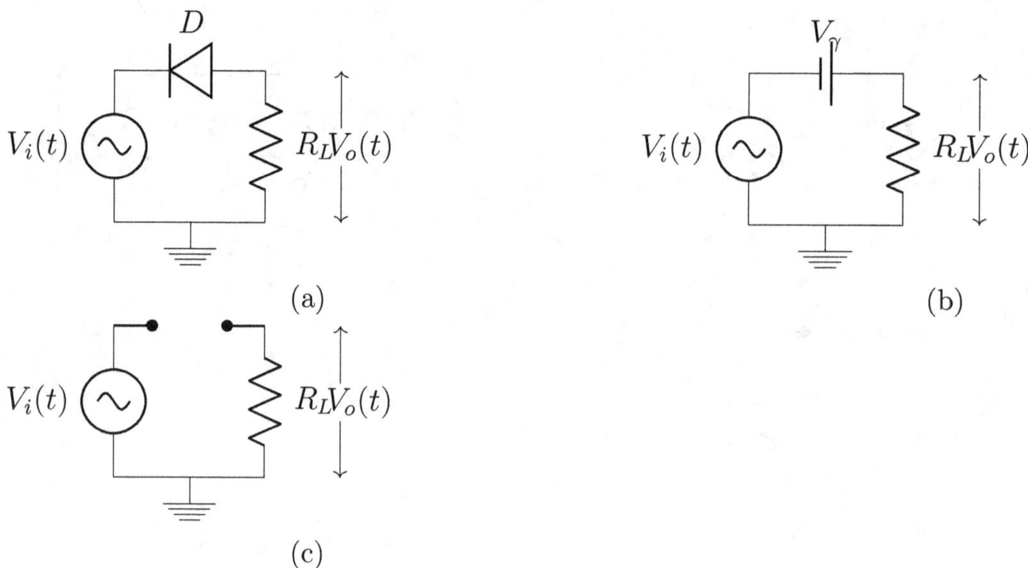

Figure 2.7: Practical diode:(a) Circuit diagram (b) when diode is forward biased (c) when diode is reverse biased

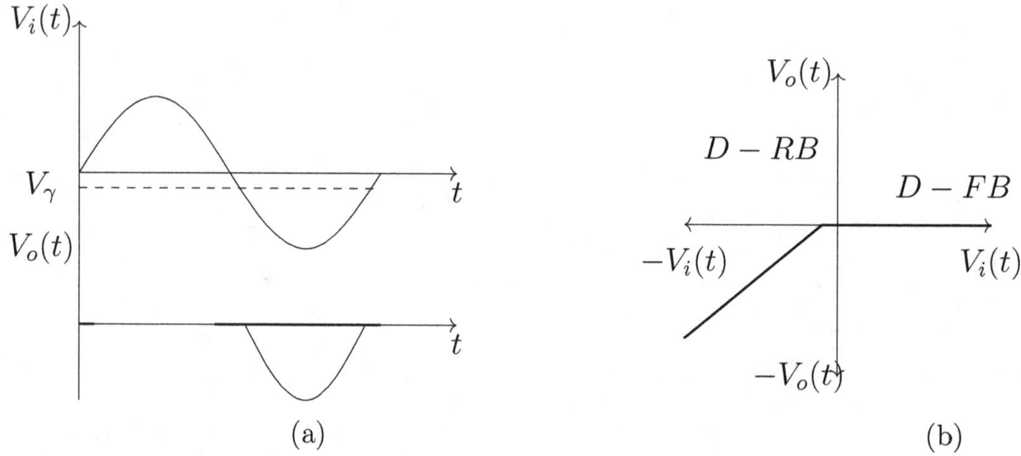

Figure 2.8: Practical diode:(a) Input and Output waveform (b) Transfer Charactersitics

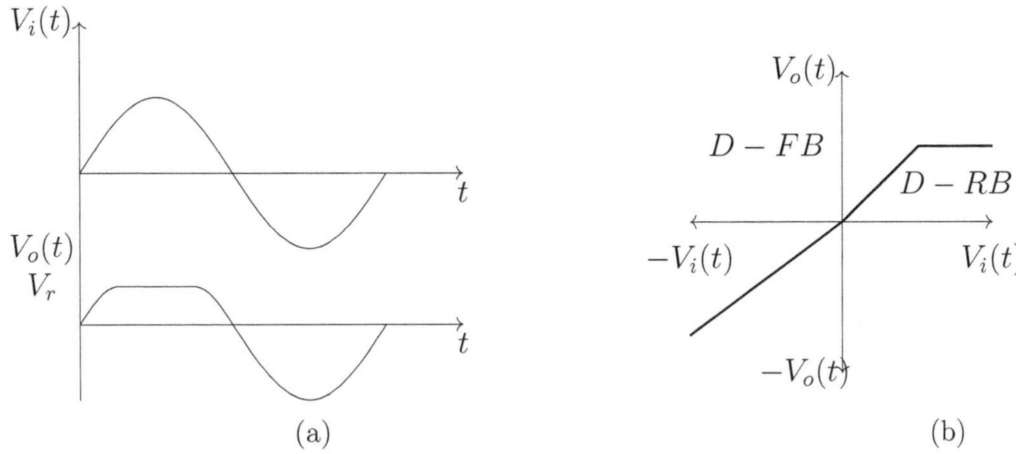

(a)   (b)

Figure 2.10: Ideal diode:(a) Input and Output waveform (b) Transfer Charactersitics

2.1.3 Biased Series Positive Clipper or Clipping above the reference voltage

The circuit diagram of Biased Series Positive Clipper or Clipping above the reference voltage is shown in the figure 2.9.

The maximum value of V_r should not exceed the maximum value of the input signal. Assuming the diode is ideal.

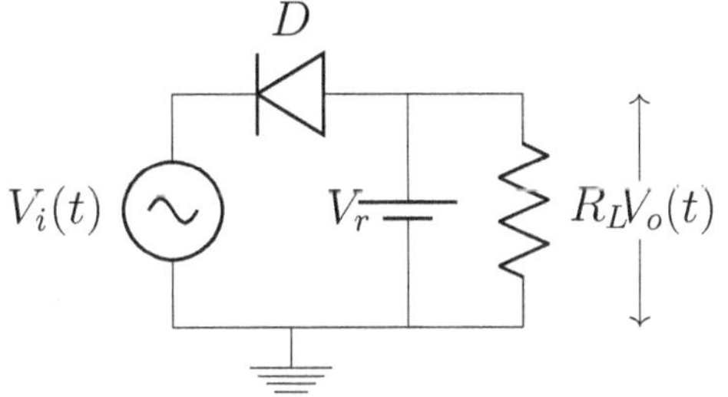

Figure 2.9: Circuit diagram of Clipping above the reference voltage

If $V_i(t) > V_r$, the diode is reverse biased and it acts as open circuit. So, the output $V_o(t) = V_r$.

If $V_i(t) < V_r$, the diode is forward biased and it acts as short circuit. So, the output $V_o(t) = V_i(t)$.

The input, Output waveforms and transfer charactersitics are shown in the figure 2.10.

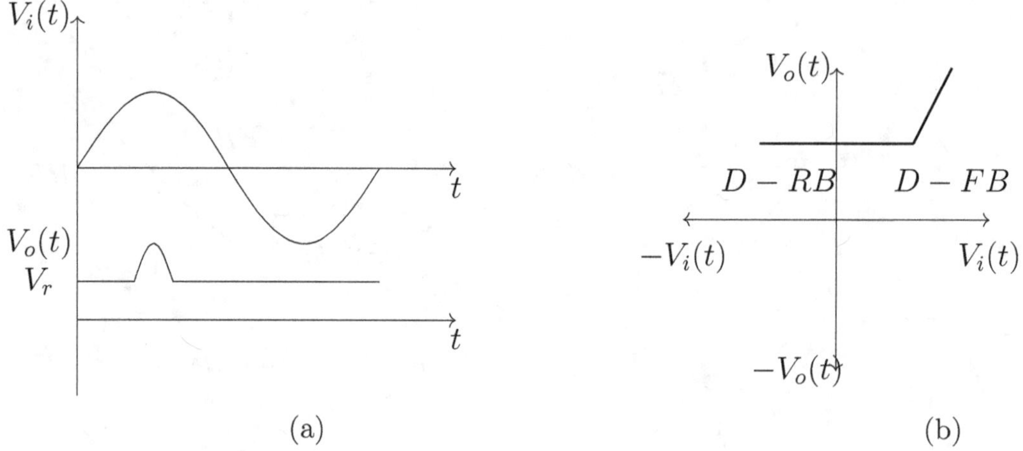

(a) (b)

Figure 2.12: Ideal diode:(a) Input and Output waveform (b) Transfer Charactersitics

2.1.4 Biased Series Negative Clipper or Clipping below the reference voltage

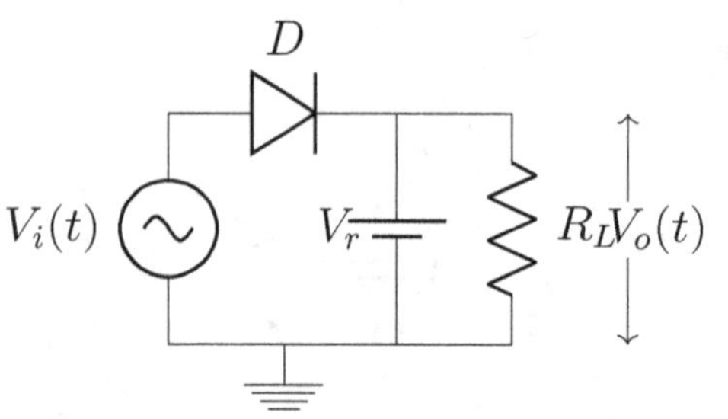

Figure 2.11: Circuit diagram of Clipping below the reference voltage

The circuit diagram of Biased Series Negative Clipper or Clipping below the reference voltage is shown in the figure 2.11.

The maximum value of V_r should not exceed the maximum value of the input signal. Assuming the diode is ideal.

If $V_i(t) > V_r$, the diode is forward biased and it acts as short circuit. So, the output $V_o(t) = V_i(t)$.

If $V_i(t) < V_r$, the diode is reverse biased and it acts as open circuit. So, the output $V_o(t) = V_r$. The input, Output waveforms and transfer charactersitics are shown in the figure 2.12.

Problem

Draw the Transfer characterstics for the circuit shown in 2.13(a). Assume diode forward resistance is 50Ω.

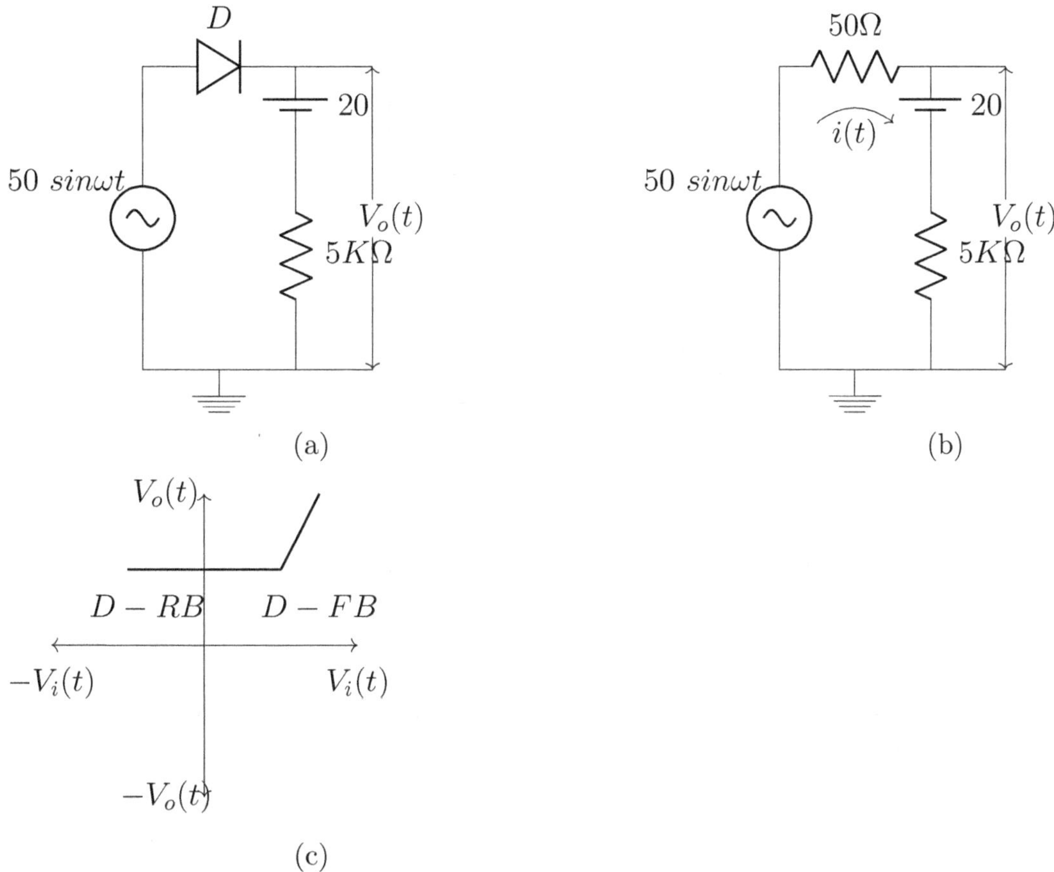

Figure 2.13: (a) circuit diagram (b) when diode is forward biased (c)transfer charactersitics

Solution

From the figure 2.13(a), it is Series Negative Clipper. The reference voltage V_r=20v. $V_i(t)$=50 $sin\omega t$.

When $V_i(t)$ <20v, the diode is reverse biased and is repalced with open circuit. So, $V_o(t)$=20v.

When $V_i(t)$ >20v, the diode is forward biased and is replaced with forward resistance 50Ω. The transfer charactersitics is shown in the figure 2.13.

$$V_o(t) = 20 + i(5 \times 10^3)$$

$$i = \frac{V_i(t) - 20}{50 + 5 \times 10^3}$$

$$= \frac{50 - 20}{50 + 5 \times 10^3} \tag{2.1}$$

$$\boxed{i = 5.94 \times 10^{-3} amps}$$

$$V_o(t) = 20 + 5.94 \times 10^{-3}(5 \times 10^3)$$

$$\boxed{V_o(t) = 49.7v}$$

2.1.5 Un-biased Negative Shunt Clippers

The circuit diagram of Un-biased Negative Shunt Clippers is shown in the figure 2.14(a). The figure 2.14(b) shows the equivalent circuit when diode is forward biased and the figure 2.14(c) shows when diode is reverse biased.

Case 1:

$V_i(t) > 0$ i.e during postive half cycle of the input, diode is reverse biased and it acts as open circuit as shown in the figure 2.14(c). Then $V_o(t) = \frac{V_i(t)R_L}{R+R_L}$. If, $R_L >> $ R, $V_o(t) = V_i(t)$.

Case 2:

$V_i(t) < 0$ i.e during negative half cycle of the input, diode is forward biased and it acts as short circuit as shown in the figure 2.14(b). Then $V_o(t)$=0.

The input, output waveforms and transfer characteristics are shown in the figure 2.15.

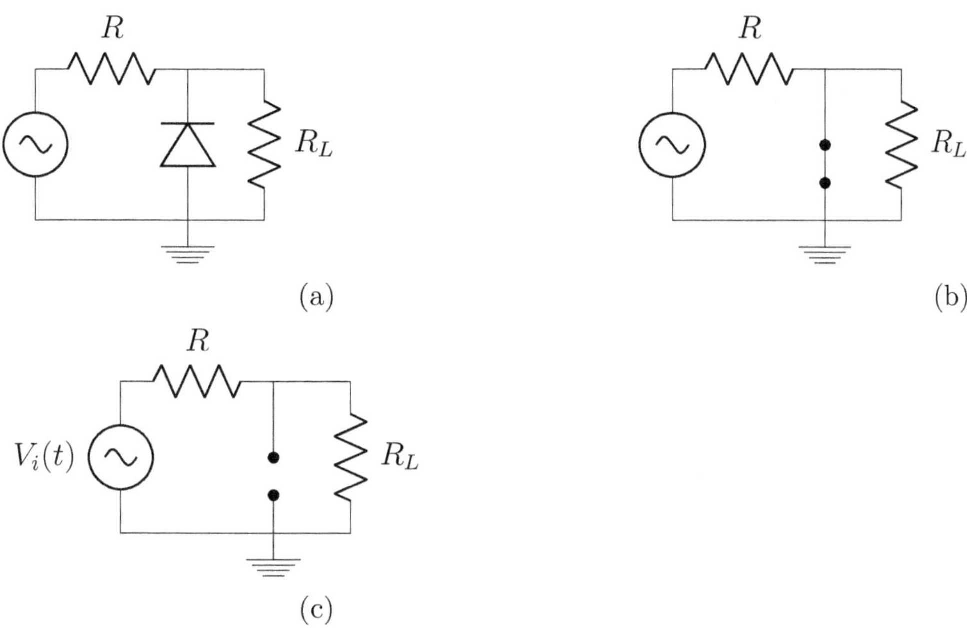

Figure 2.14: (a) Circuit diagram (b) diode forward biased (c) diode reverse biased

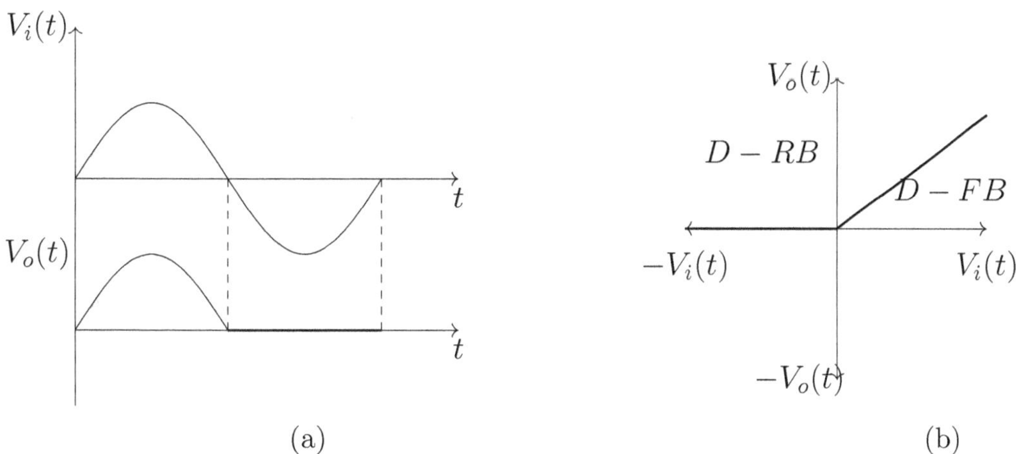

Figure 2.15: Un-biased Negative Shunt Clippers:(a) Input and Output waveform (b) Transfer Charactersitics

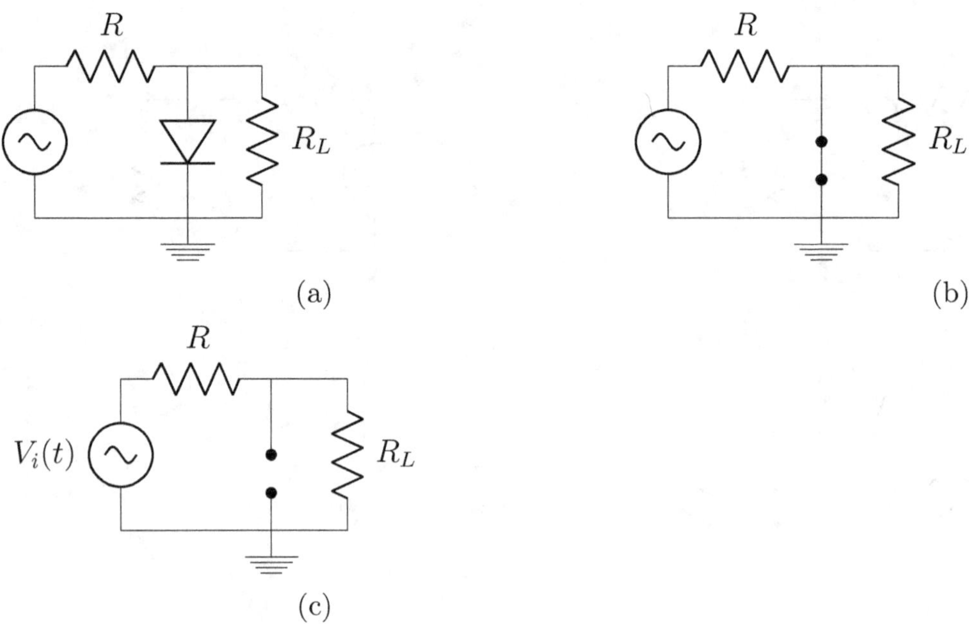

Figure 2.16: Un-biased Positive Shunt Clippers(a) Circuit diagram (b) diode forward biased (c) diode reverse biased

2.1.6 Un-biased Positive Shunt Clippers

The circuit diagram of Un-biased Positive Shunt Clippers is shown in the figure 2.16(a). The figure 2.16(b) shows the equivalent circuit when diode is forward biased and the figure 2.16(c) shows when diode is reverse biased.

Case 1:

$V_i(t) > 0$ i.e during postive half cycle of the input, diode is forward biased and it acts as short circuit as shown in the figure 2.14(b). Then $V_o(t)=0$.

Case 2:

$V_i(t) < 0$ i.e during negative half cycle of the input, diode is reverse biased and it acts as open circuit as shown in the figure 2.14(c). Then $V_o(t) = \frac{V_i(t)R_L}{R+R_L}$. If, $R_L >> R$, $V_o(t) = V_i(t)$.

The input, output waveforms and transfer characteristics are shown in the figure 2.17.

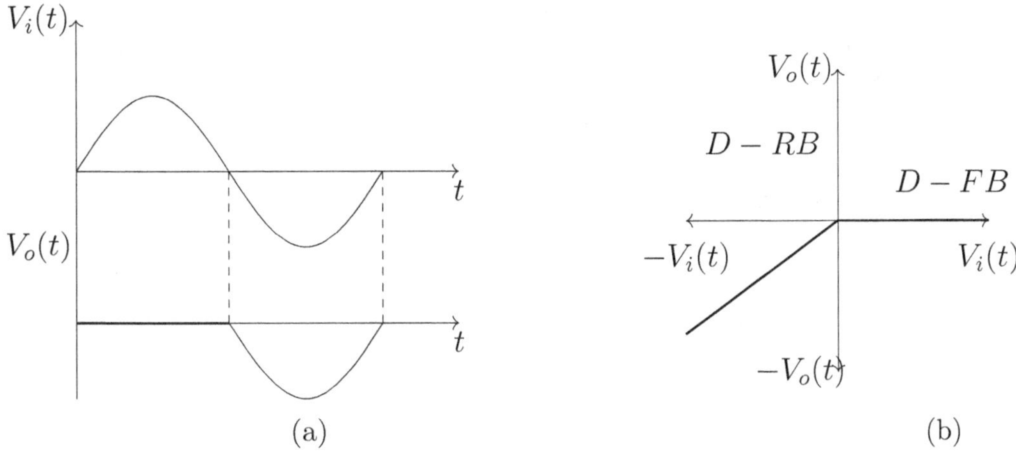

Figure 2.17: Un-biased Positive Shunt Clipper:(a) Input and Output waveform (b) Transfer Charactersitics

2.1.7 Biased Positive Shunt Clipper

The circuit diagram of biased Positive Shunt Clippers is shown in the figure 2.18(a). The figure 2.18(b) shows the equivalent circuit when diode is forward biased and the figure 2.18(c) shows when diode is reverse biased.

Case 1:

If $V_i(t) > V_r$ i.e during postive half cycle, the diode is forward biased and it acts as short circuit which is shown in the figure 2.18(b), then $V_o(t) = V_r$.

Case 2:

If $V_i(t) < V_r$ i.e during negative half cycle, the diode is reverse biased and it acts as open circuit which is shown in the figure 2.18(c), then $V_o(t) = \frac{V_i(t)R_L}{R+R_L}$. If, $R_L >> R$, $V_o(t) = V_i(t)$.

The input, output waveforms and transfer characteristics are shown in the figure 2.19.

2.1.8 Biased Negative Shunt Clipper

The circuit diagram of biased Negative Shunt Clippers is shown in the figure 2.20(a). The figure 2.20(b) shows the equivalent circuit when diode is forward biased and the figure 2.20(c) shows when diode is reverse biased.

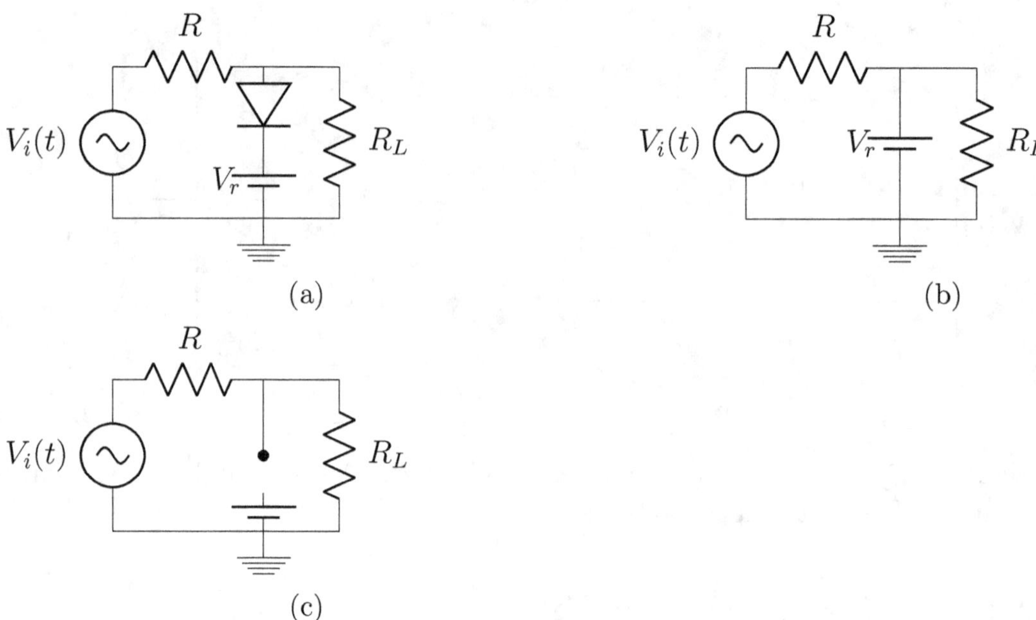

Figure 2.18: biased Positive Shunt Clippers(a) Circuit diagram (b) diode forward biased (c) diode reverse biased

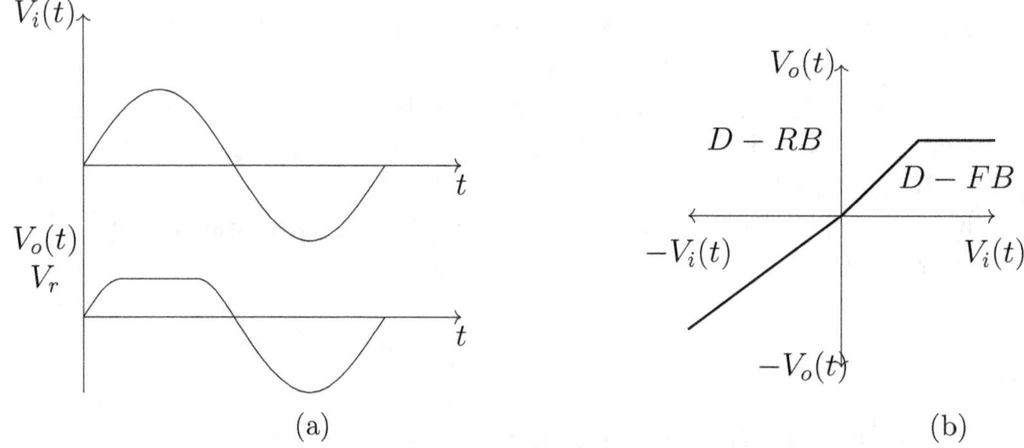

Figure 2.19: biased Positive Shunt Clippers:(a) Input and Output waveform (b) Transfer Charactersitics

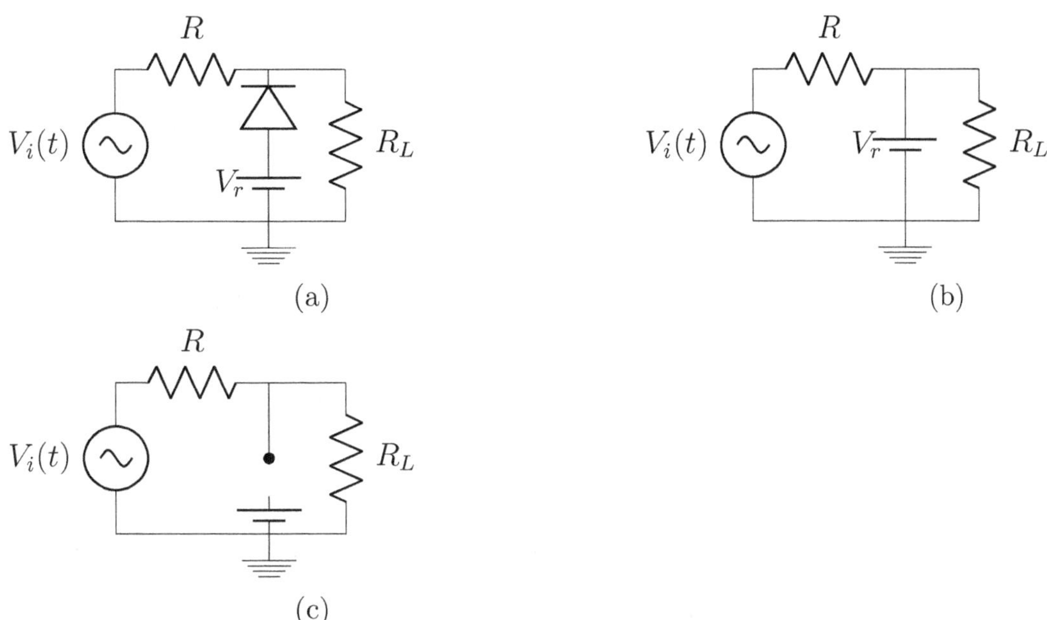

Figure 2.20: biased negative Shunt Clippers(a) Circuit diagram (b) diode forward biased (c) diode reverse biased

Case 1: If $V_i(t) > V_r$ i.e during postive half cycle, the diode is reverse biased and it acts as open circuit which is shown in the figure 2.20(c), then $V_o(t) = \frac{V_i(t)R_L}{R+R_L}$. If, $R_L >> R$, $V_o(t) = V_i(t)$.

Case 2:

If $V_i(t) < V_r$ i.e during negative half cycle, the diode is forward biased and it acts as short circuit which is shown in the figure 2.18(b), then $V_o(t)=0$..

The input, output waveforms and transfer characteristics are shown in the figure 2.21.

2.1.9 Two Level Clipper

It is a circuit which removes portions of both positive and negative half cycle of the input. The circuit diagram is shown in the figure 2.22. The magnitude of V_1 and V_2 must be lie between $V_i(t)$.

Case 1: During Positive Half Cycle

Diode D_2 is completely reverse biased.

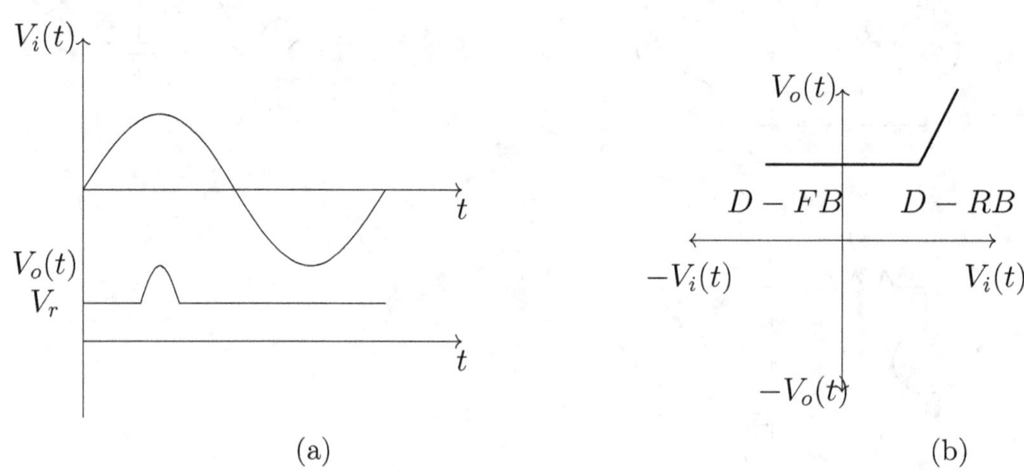

Figure 2.21: biased negative Shunt Clippers:(a) Input and Output waveform (b) Transfer Charactersitics

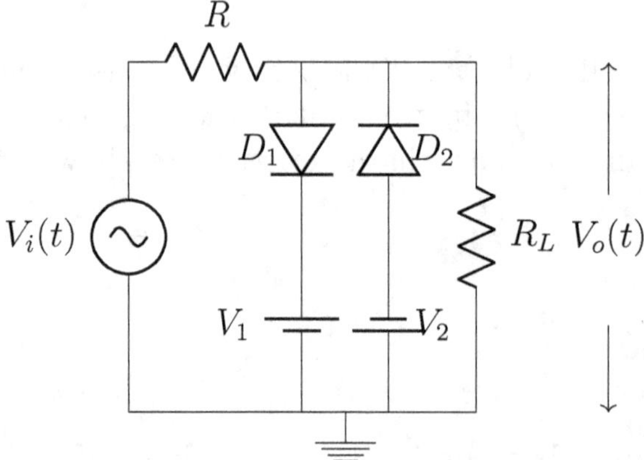

Figure 2.22: Two Level Clipper

Case 1(a):
When $V_i > V_1$, Diode D_1 is forward biased and it acts as short circuit.
The output

$$\boxed{V_o(t) = V_1}\tag{2.2}$$

Case 1(b):
When $V_i < V_1$, Diode D_1 is reverse biased and it acts as open circuit.
The output

$$\boxed{V_o(t) = \frac{V_i \times R_L}{R + R_L}}\tag{2.3}$$

If $R_L >> R$,

$$\boxed{V_o(t) = V_i(t)}\tag{2.4}$$

The circuit diagram is shown in the figure 2.23

Case 2: During Negative Half Cycle

Diode D_1 is completely reverse biased and is replaced with open circuit.
The circuit diagram is shown in the figure 2.24.

Case 2(a)
When $V_i > V_2$, Diode D_2 is reverse biased and acts as open circuit, Then
output

$$\boxed{V_o(t) = \frac{V_i \times R_L}{R + R_L}}\tag{2.5}$$

If $R_L >> R$,

$$\boxed{V_o(t) = V_i(t)}\tag{2.6}$$

Case 2(b)
When $V_i < V_2$, Diode D_2 is forward biased and acts as short circuit, Then
output

$$\boxed{V_o(t) = V_2}\tag{2.7}$$

Output waveform The output waveform of two level clipper is shown in
the figure 2.25

Problems

1. Draw the transfer characteristics for the circuit shown in 2.26(a).

   Solution:

   Assuming both the diodes are ideal.

   Case 1: During positive half cycle of the input

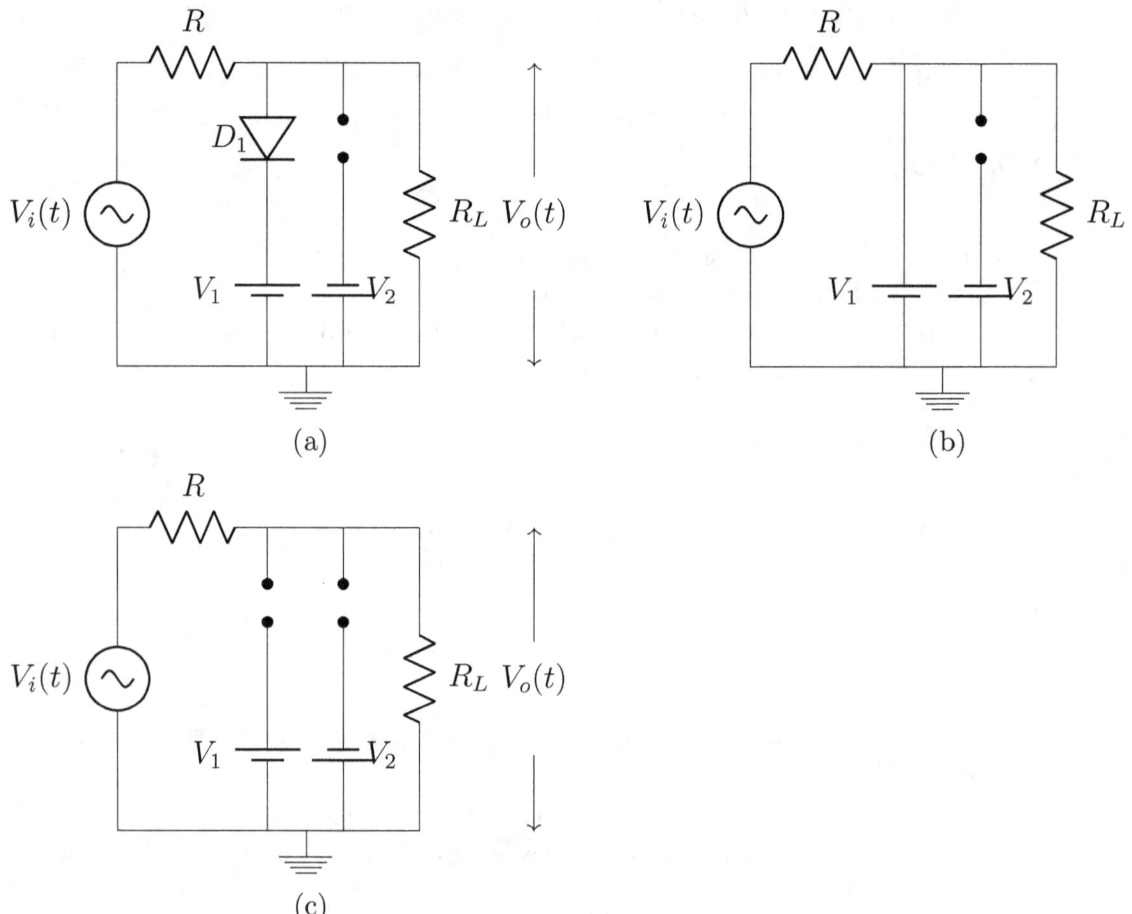

Figure 2.23: Two level Clipper : (a) D_2 reverse biased (b) D_1 forward biased (c) D_1 reverse biased

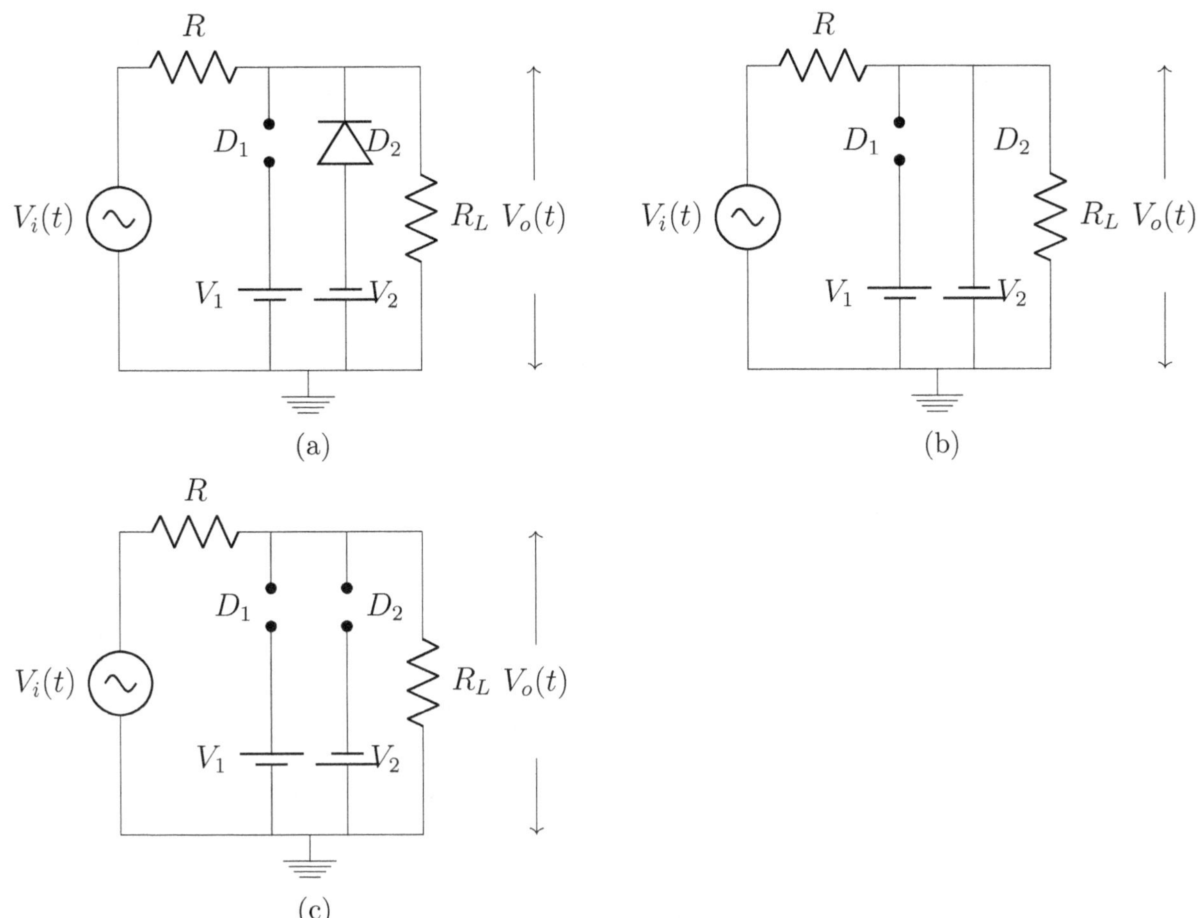

Figure 2.24: Two Level Clipper: (a) D_1 reverse biased (b) D_2 forward biased (c) D_3 reverse biased

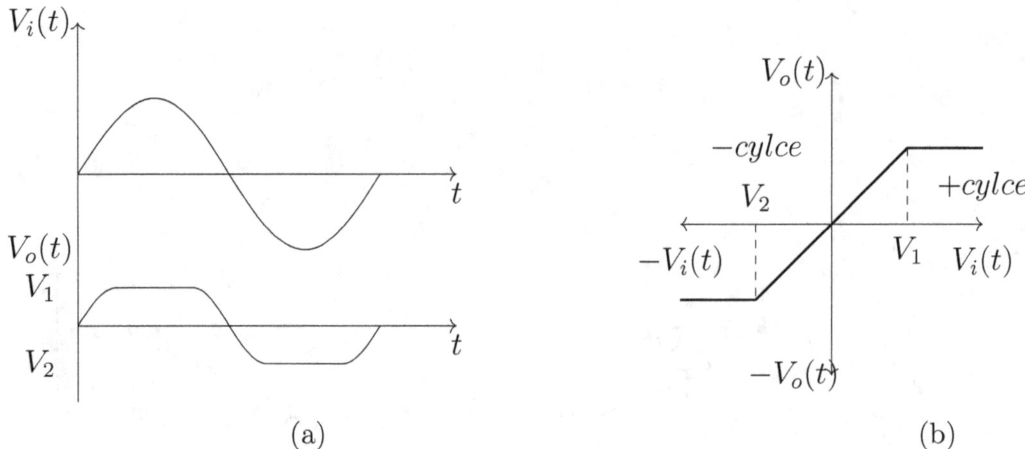

Figure 2.25: Two Level Clipper:(a) Input and Output waveform (b) Transfer Charactersitics

Diode D_2 is completley reverse biased, Diode D_1 is completley forward biased.

When $V_i(t) > 0$, D_1 is replaced with short circuit, D_2 is replaced with open circuit. The circuit diagram is shown in the figure 2.26(b).

$$V_o(t) = \frac{V_i \times 1 \times 10^3}{1 \times 10^3 + 1 \times 10^3} \quad V_o(t) = \frac{V_i}{2} \tag{2.8}$$

Case 2: During negative half cycle of the input

Diode D_1 is completley reverse biased, Diode D_2 is completley forward biased.

When $V_i(t) < 0$, D_2 is replaced with short circuit, D_1 is replaced with open circuit. The circuit diagram is shown in the figure 2.26(c). The transfer characteristics is shown in the figure 2.27.

$$V_o(t) = \frac{V_i \times 1 \times 10^3}{1 \times 10^3 + 1 \times 10^3} \quad V_o(t) = \frac{V_i}{2} \tag{2.9}$$

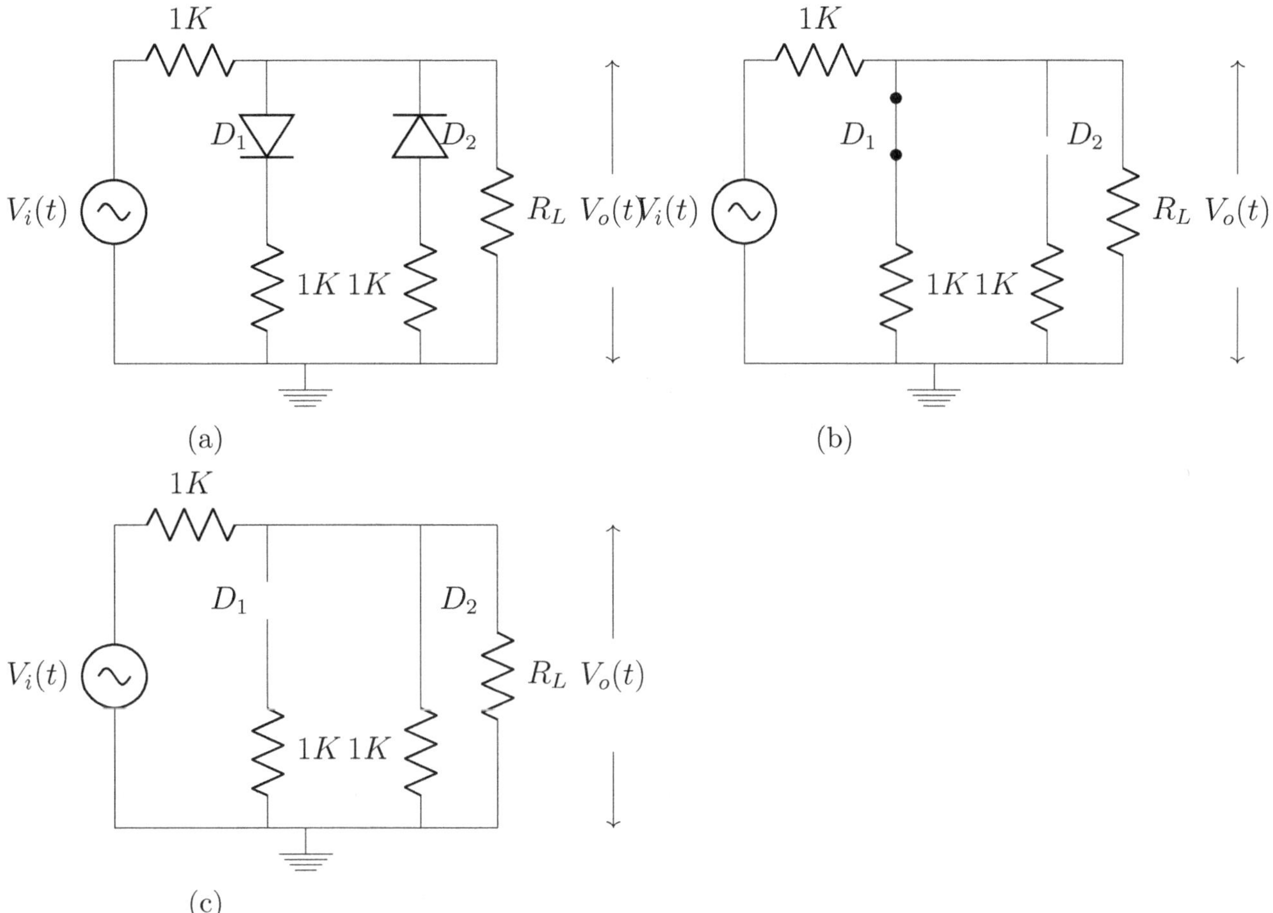

Figure 2.26: (a) Circuit diagram (b) D_1FB, D_2RB(c)D_1RB, D_2FB (d) Transfer characterisitcs

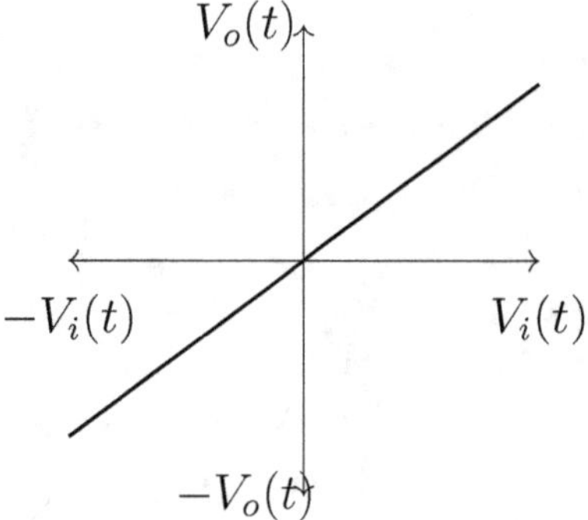

Figure 2.27: Transfer Charactersitics

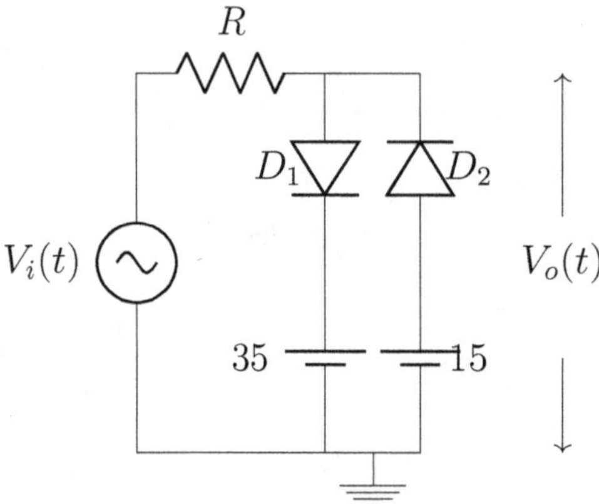

Figure 2.28: Problem2:Two Level Clipper

2. Draw the transfer characterisitcs of the circuit shown in the figure 2.28

Solution:

Case 1: $V_i > 35$

During this case, diode D_1 is forward biased which acts as short circuit and D_2 is reverse biased which is replaced with open circuit. Then output $V_o = 35$v.

Case 2: $15 < V_i < 35$

During this case, both the diodes D_1 i and D_2 are reverse biased which are replaced with open circuit. Then output $V_o = V_i$.

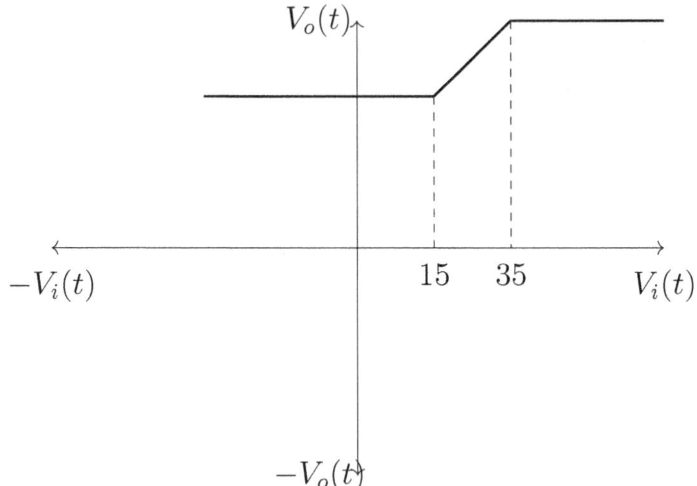

Figure 2.29: Problem2: Transfer Charactersitics

Case 2: V_i <15

During this case, diode D_2 is forward biased which acts as short circuit and D_1 is reverse biased which is replaced with open circuit. Then output V_o=15v.

The transfer characterisitcs are shown in the figure 2.29.

2.2 Emitter Coupled Clipper

The circuit of Emitter Coupled Clipper is shown in the figure 2.30 where the sinusoidal input is connected to the base of the transistor T_1 and a fixed DC voltage is applied to the base of the transistor T_2.When the voltage at base wrt emitter i.e $V_{be} > 0.7$, the transistor operates in saturation region and if the voltage at base wrt emitter i.e $V_{be} < 0.7$, the transistor operates in cut-off region. If the input voltage $V_i < 0$, the transistor T_1 will be in cut-off state but the transistor T_2 operates in active region because of the fixed DC voltage applied to the base of the transistor T_2. Then the output voltage $V_o = V_{cc} - i_{c2}R_{c2}$.When the input voltage increases both the transistors will operate in active region and the output voltage $V_o \propto V_i$. When the input voltage is further increased, there will be current from both the emitter terminals. As the voltage drop across the emitter resistor R_e

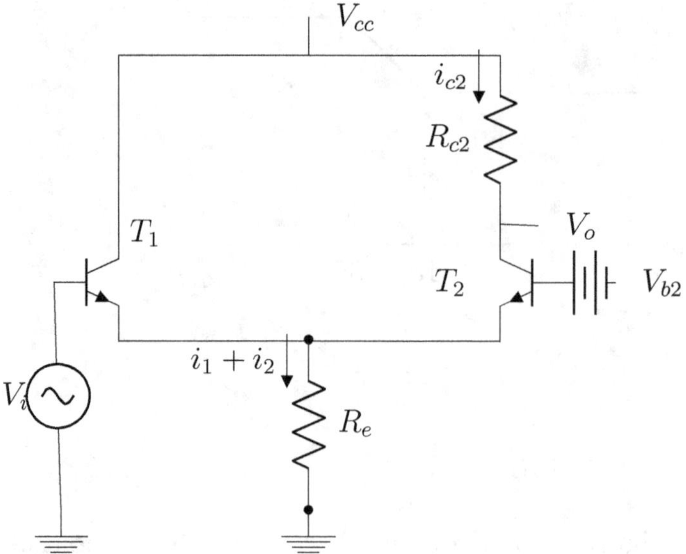

Figure 2.30: Emitter Coupled Clipper

increases which makes the transistor T_2 to change from active region to cut-off region. Then the output voltage $V_o = V_{cc}$. The transfer characteristics of Emitter Coupled Clipper is shown in the figure 2.31.

2.3   Clampers

It is a circuit which adds DC voltage to output signal. There are two types of clampers:

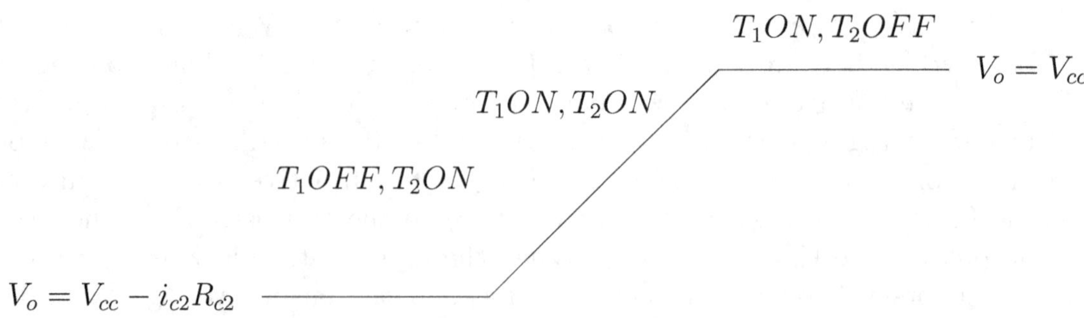

Figure 2.31: Transfer characteristics of Emitter Coupled Clipper

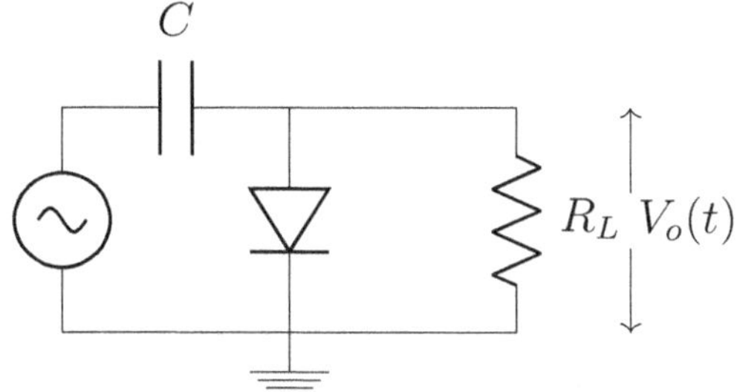

Figure 2.32: Negative Clamper

1. Negative Clampers

2. Positve Clampers

2.3.1   Negative Clamper or Positive peak clamper

The circuit of Negative Clamper or Positive peak clamper is shown in the figure 2.32.

Steps to anlayse a clamper

1. Identify for which cylce of the input, diode gets forward biased.

2. Capacitor charges only when diode is forward biased.

3. Represent the flow of current.

4. Represent polarity across capacitor based on the flow of current.

5. Apply KVL to find the output expression.

6. Draw the output waveform.

For the circuit shown in the figure 2.32, diode gets forward biased during postive half cylce of the input i.e $V_i(t) > 0$. So, the represntation of current is shown in the figure 2.33. By applying KVL, the ouput $V_o(t) = V_i(t) - V_c$, where V_c is the voltage available at the capacitor which is equal to the maximum postive input voltage i.e V_m since capacitor charges during positive half cylce of the input.

since $V_i(t)$ is a sinusoidal signal, for different voltages the output is given as: $V_0(t) = V_i(t) - V_m$. The input and waveformis shown in the figure 2.34. For different values of input voltages, output voltage is given as

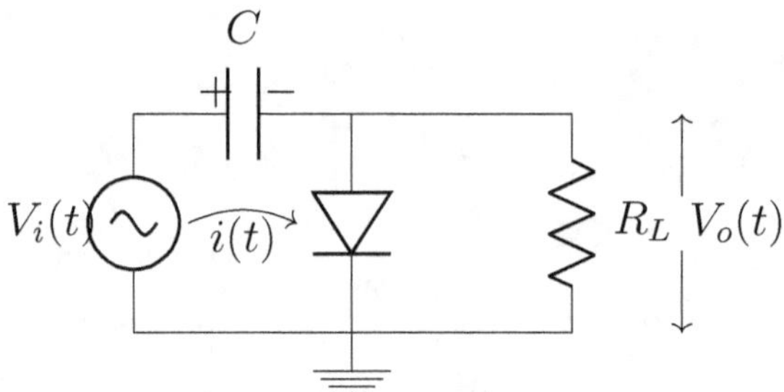

Figure 2.33: Negative Clamper1

- When $V_i(t)=0$, $V_0(t)=-V_m$

- When $V_i(t)=V_m$, $V_0(t)=0$

- When $V_i(t)=-V_m$, $V_0(t)=-2 \times V_m$

2.3.2   Positive Clamper or Negative peak clamper

The circuit of Positive Clamper or Negative peak clamper is shown in the figure 2.35.

Steps to anlayse a clamper

1. Identify for which cylce of the input, diode gets forward biased.

2. Capacitor charges only when diode is forward biased.

3. Represent the direction of flow of current.

4. Represent polarity across capacitor based on the flow of current.

5. Apply KVL to find the output expression.

6. Draw the output waveform.

For the circuit shown in the figure 2.35, diode gets forward biased during negatice half cycle of the input i.e $V_i(t) < 0$. So, the representation of current is shown in the figure 2.36. By applying KVL, the ouput $V_o(t) = V_i(t) + V_c$, where V_c is the voltage available at the capacitor which is equal to the maximum postive input voltage i.e V_m since capacitor charges during positive half cylce of the input.

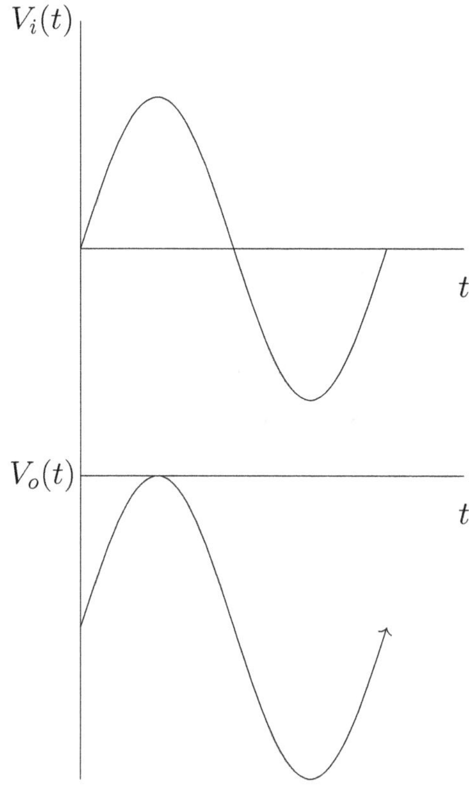

Figure 2.34: Negative Clamper: Input-Output waveform

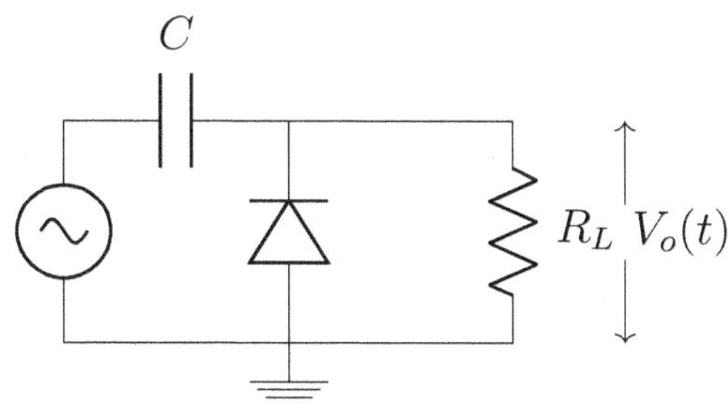

Figure 2.35: Positive Clamper

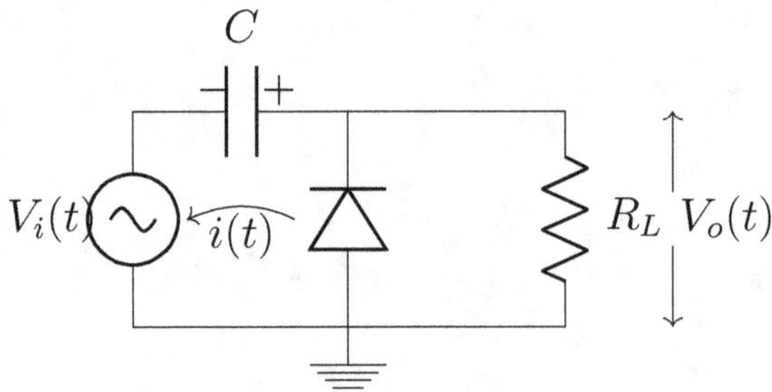

Figure 2.36: Positive Clamper1

since $V_i(t)$ is a sinusoidal signal, for different voltages the output is given as: $V_0(t) = V_i(t) + V_m$. The input and waveformis shown in the figure 2.37. For different values of input voltages, output voltage is given as

- When $V_i(t)=0$, $V_0(t)=V_m$

- When $V_i(t)=V_m$, $V_0(t)= 2 \times V_m$

- When $V_i(t)=-V_m$, $V_0(t)=0$

2.4   Clamping Circuit Theorem

Statement Under steady state conditions the ratio of the area of the output curve during forward biased to the area of the output curve during reverse biased is given as

$$\boxed{\frac{A_f}{A_r} = \frac{R_f}{R}}$$
(2.10)

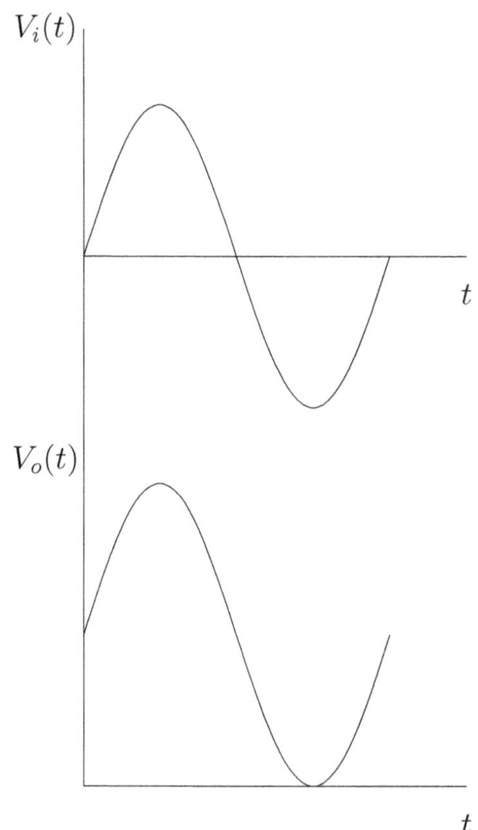

Figure 2.37: Positive Clamper: Input-Output waveform

Proof

$$Charge\,Q_{gain} = \int_0^{T_1} I_f dt$$

$$= \frac{1}{R_f} \int_0^{T_1} V_o(t) dt$$

$$= \frac{A_f}{R_f}$$

$$Charge\,Q_{lost} = \int_{T_1}^{T_2} I_r dt$$

$$= \frac{1}{R} \int_{T_1}^{T_2} V_o(t) dt \qquad (2.11)$$

$$= \frac{A_r}{R}$$

$$Q_{gain} = Q_{lost}$$

$$\boxed{\frac{A_f}{A_r} = \frac{R_f}{R}}$$

2.5   Design of Clamper Circuit

Let R_f is forward resistance and R_r is reverse resistance of diaode, R is calculated as

$$R = \sqrt{R_f \times R_r}$$

$$RC = 20 \times T \qquad (2.12)$$

where R_f=100 Ω and R_r=100KΩ and T is the time period of the input waveform.

Chapter 3

Multivibrators

Multivibrators are the circuits which produces the signals with multiple frequencies. These are also called as Regenerate Amplifiers. Based on the feedback, multivibrators are classified into three types:

- Bistable Multivibrator: It has two stable states. It requires two trigerring signals to change from one stable to another stable state. It is also called as Flip-flop or Binary.

- Monostable Multivibrator: It has one stable state and one quasi stable state. Quasi stable state means ouptut remains in a partcular state only for a particular time period. So, it requires only one triggering signal to change from stable state to quasi stable state. It is also called as One shot Multivibrator.

- Astable Multivibrator: It has two quasi stable states. So no trigerring signal is required. It is also called as Free running multivibrator.

3.1 Bistable Multivibrator

It is the circuit which has two stable states. It is also called as Flip-flop. Since it is having two stable states, it requires two triggering pulses to change the output from one state to another. The triggering may be postive or negative.

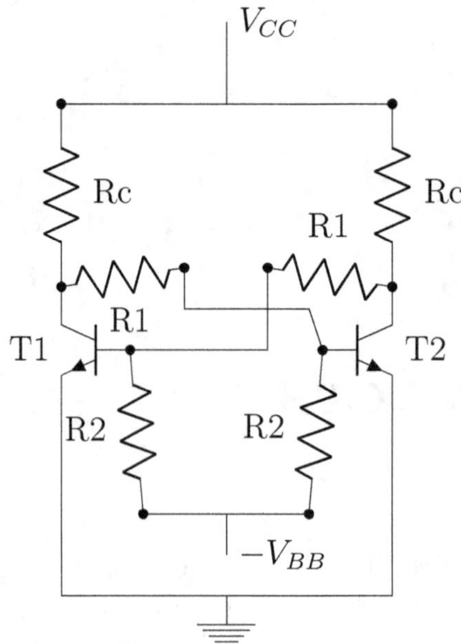

Figure 3.1: Collector Coupled Bistable Multivibrator

3.1.1   Fixed bias Bistable Multivibrator

The circuit diagram of Fixed bias Bistable Multivibrator is shown in 3.1 Transistors T_1 and T_2 are both indentical NPN transistors. The collector of T_1 is connected to base of T_2 with a resistor and similarly collector of T_2 is connected to base of T_1 with a resistor. Fixed negative bias is provided to the resistors connected to both base terminals.

Even though both the transistors are identical, they may not exhibit same property at a time. So, initially assuming transistor T_1 is in cut off and transistor T_2 is in saturation. Then $V_{CE_1} = V_{CC}$ and $V_{CE_2} = V_{CE_{sat}}$. This is first stable state.

If a negative triggering pulse is applied to base of T_2 or collector of T_1, transisor T_2 will be in cut off and transistor T_1 will be in saturation. Then, $V_{CE_2} = V_{CC}$ and $V_{CE_1} = V_{CE_{sat}}$. This is second stable state.

Since this circuit requires two triggering pulses it is also called as Flip-flop. The ouptut wave forms are shown in the figure 3.2.

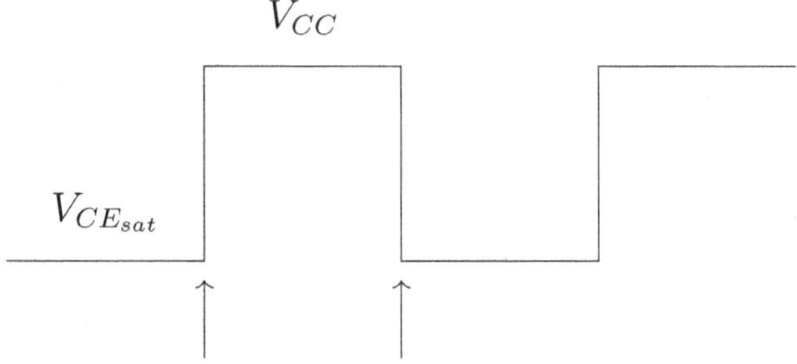

Figure 3.2: Output waveoforms of Bistable Multivibrator considering T_2 will be in cut off and transistor T_1 will be in saturation

3.1.2 Probelms

1. A fixed bias binary uses NPN transistors V_{CEsat} =0.5V, $V_{BEcutoff}$=0. The circuit parameters are V_{CC}=V_{BB}=6V, $R_C = 1K\Omega$, $R_1 = 4.7K\Omega$,$R_2 = 27K\Omega$. Find $hfe(min)$ and stable voltages, currents.

Solution
The circuit diagram with voltage and current representations are shown in the figure 3.3. Assuming initally T_1 is OFF and T_2 is ON.

Given parameters:

V_{CEsat} =0.5V, $V_{BEcutoff}$=0, V_{CC}=V_{BB}=6V, $R_C = 1K\Omega$, $R_1 = 4.7K\Omega$,$R_2 = 27K\Omega$

$$\begin{aligned}
I_1 &= \frac{V_{CC} - V_{CEsat}}{R_C} \\
&= \frac{6 - 0.5}{1.2K\Omega} \\
&= 4.5mA \\
I_2 &= \frac{V_{CEsat} - (-V_{BB})}{R_1 + R_2} \\
&= \frac{0.5 + 6}{4.7K\Omega + 27K\Omega} \\
&= 0.205mA
\end{aligned} \qquad (3.1)$$

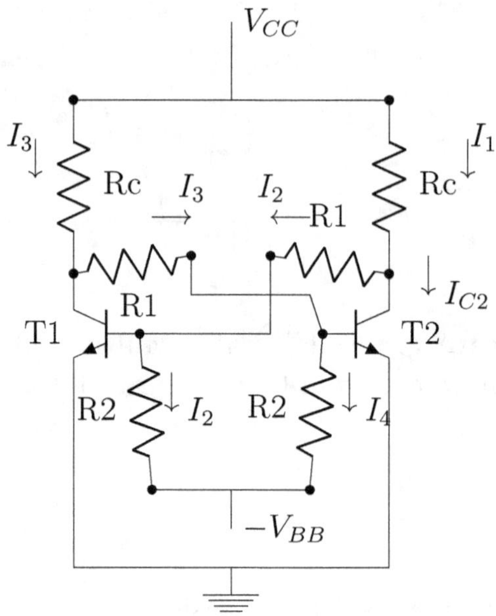

Figure 3.3: Problem 1: Circuit Diagram

From the circuit diagram 3.3

$$I_1 = I_2 + I_{C2}$$
$$4.5mA = 0.205mA + I_{C2}$$
$$I_{C2} = 4.29mA$$
$$I_3 = \frac{V_{CC} - V_{BE_{sat}}}{R_C + R_1}$$
$$= \frac{6 - 1}{1.2K\Omega + 4.7K\Omega}$$
$$= 0.84mA$$
$$I_4 = \frac{V_{BE_{sat}} - (-V_{BB})}{R_2} \qquad (3.2)$$
$$= \frac{1 + 6}{27K\Omega}$$
$$= 0.26mA$$
$$I_3 = I_4 + I_{B2}$$
$$0.84mA = 0.26mA + I_{B2}$$
$$I_{B2} = 0.58mA$$
$$V_{C1} = V_{CC} - I_3 \times R_C$$
$$= 5V$$

$$V_{B1} = V_{CE_{sat}} - I_2 \times R_1$$
$$= -0.46V$$
$$hfe = \frac{I_{C2}}{I_{B2}} \tag{3.3}$$
$$= 7.75$$

Steps to design Fixed bias binary (Bistable Multivibrator)

- $I_1 = I_{C2}$

- $I_{C2} = 5\text{mA}$

- $I_B = \frac{I_C}{hfe(min)}$

- $I_{B_{actual}} = 1.5 \times I_B$

- $I_4 = \frac{1}{10} I_{C2}$

2. Design a fixed bias binary with supply voltages 12v. Assume $hfe(min)=50$ for the circuit diagram 3.3.

Solution

Considering the assumptions in designing the fixed binary from the circuit diagram 3.3

$$R_C = \frac{V_{CC} - V_{CE}}{I_1}$$
$$= \frac{12 - 0.2}{5m}$$
$$= 2.35K\Omega$$

$$I_4 = \frac{1}{10} I_{C2}$$
$$= 0.5mA$$

$$R_2 = \frac{V_{BE} - (-V_{BB})}{I_4}$$
$$= \frac{0.6 + 12}{0.5m}$$
$$= 25.2K\Omega$$

$$I_B = \frac{I_C}{hfe(min)}$$
$$= \frac{5m}{50}$$
$$= 0.1mA$$

$$I_{B_{actual}} = 1.5 \times I_B$$
$$= 0.15mA \tag{3.4}$$

$$I_3 = I_4 + I_{B_{actual}}$$
$$= 0.65mA$$

$$I_3 = \frac{V_{CC} - V_{B2}}{R_1 + R - C}$$
$$0.65m = \frac{12 - 0.6}{R_1 + 2.35K\Omega}$$
$$R_1 = 15.2K\Omega$$

$$I_2 = \frac{V_{C2} - (-V_{BB})}{R_1 + R_2}$$
$$= \frac{0.2 + 12}{15K\Omega + 25.2K\Omega}$$
$$= 0.3mA$$

$$V_{C1} = V_{CC} - I_3 \times R_C$$
$$= 12 - (0.65m)(2.35K\Omega)$$
$$= 10.47V$$

$$V_{B1} = V_{C2} - I_2 \times R_2$$
$$= 0.2 - (0.3m)(25.2K\Omega)$$
$$= -7.36V$$

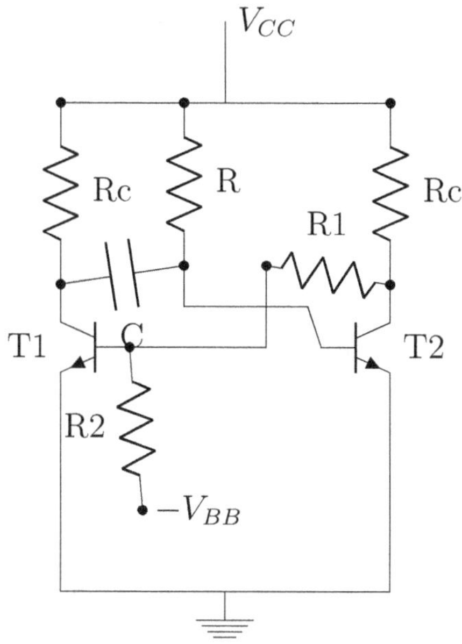

Figure 3.4: Collector Coupled Monostable Multivibrator

3.2 Monostable Multivibrator

It has one stable state and one quasi stable state. Quasi stable state means ouptut remains in a partcular state only for a particular time period. So, it requires only one triggering signal to change from stable state to quasi stable state. It is also called as One shot Multivibrator. The circuit daigram is shown in the figure 3.4 Assuming intially T_2 is ON and T_1 is OFF. Then $V_{C1} = V_{CC}$ and $V_{C2} = V_{CE_{sat}}$. This state is called Stable State.

When a negative tirggering signal is applied to base of transistor T_2, T_2 will in OFF state and T_1 will be in ON state. Then $V_{C2} = V_{CC}$ and $V_{C1} = V_{CE_{sat}}$. During this period the capacitor charges through $V_{CC}, R, T_1 ON$. When the voltage at base of T_2 is greater than the $V_{BE_{sat}}$, transistor T_2 will be ON and transistor T_1 will be in OFF state. This state is called Quasi stable state.

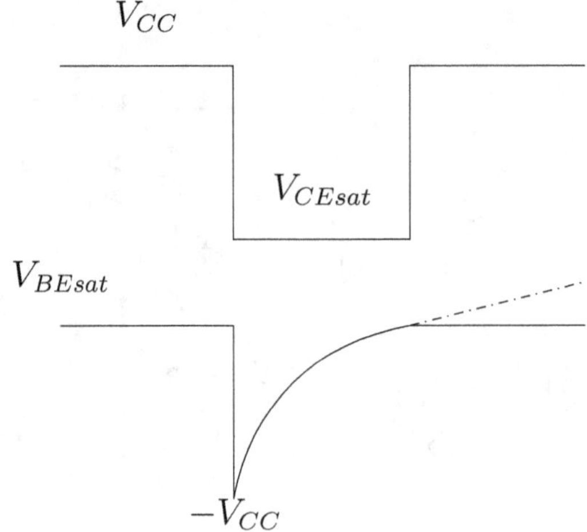

Figure 3.5: Output waveform

3.2.1   Expression for Gate width

Gate width is defined as how much time does monostable multivibrator will remain in Quasi stable stae.

Consider the waveforms shown in the figure 3.5 for calculating gate width. Cosidering the expression

$$V_o = V_f + (V_i - V_f)e^{\frac{-t}{RC}}$$

$$V_{BE_{sat}} = V_{CC} + (-V_{CC} - V_{CC})e^{\frac{-t}{RC}}$$

$$0 = V_{CC} - 2V_{CC}e^{\frac{-t}{RC}}$$

$$\frac{1}{2} = e^{\frac{-t}{RC}} \tag{3.5}$$

$$\ln(0.5) = \frac{-t}{RC}$$

$$\boxed{t = 0.69RC}$$

3.2.2   Application of Monostable multivibrator as Voltage to Time Converter

The very improtant application of Monostable multivibrator is Voltage to Time Converter. The modified circuit diagram is shown in the figure 3.6

where by changing the voltage, time varies. So a variable voltage is introduced in the circuit diagram.

$$V_o = V_f + (V_i - V_f)e^{\frac{-t}{RC}}$$

$$V_{BE_{sat}} = V + (-V_{CC} - V)e^{\frac{-t}{RC}}$$

$$0 = V - V_{CC}e^{\frac{-t}{RC}} - Ve^{\frac{-t}{RC}}$$

$$= V - [V_{CC} + V]e^{\frac{-t}{RC}}$$

$$[V_{CC} + V]e^{\frac{-t}{RC}} = V$$

$$e^{\frac{-t}{RC}} = \frac{V}{V_{CC} + V} \qquad (3.6)$$

$$\frac{-t}{RC} = \ln[\frac{V}{V_{CC} + V}]$$

$$-t = RC\ln[\frac{V}{V_{CC} + V}]$$

$$t = RC\ln[\frac{V_{CC} + V}{V}]$$

$$\boxed{t = RC\ln[1 + \frac{V_{CC}}{V}]}$$

Problem

Design a collector coupled one shot multivibrator with a gate width of 3ms.

Solution Let $h_{fe}min=20$, $R_1=R_2$, $V_{cc}=6$V, $I_c(sat)=2$mA. The circuit

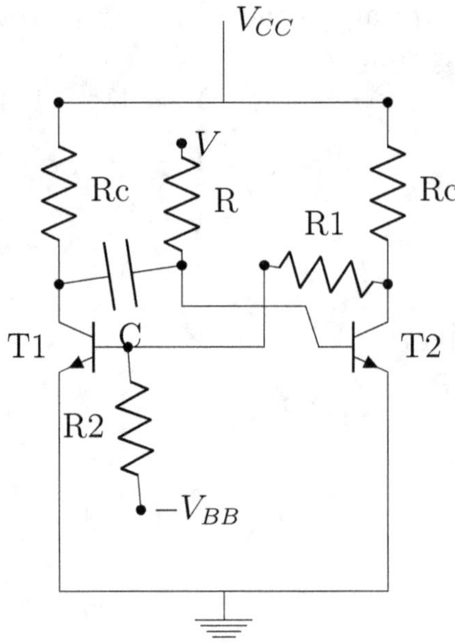

Figure 3.6: Application of Monostable Multivibrator

diagram is shown in the figure 3.4.

$$R_c = \frac{V_{cc} - V_{ce}}{I_c(sat)}$$

$$= \frac{6 - 0}{2}$$

$$= 3k\Omega$$

$$I_{b2}(min) = \frac{I_c(sat)}{h_{fe}min}$$

$$= \frac{2}{20}$$

$$= 0.1mA$$

$$R = \frac{V_{cc} - V_{ce}}{I_b} \tag{3.7}$$

$$= \frac{6}{0.15}$$

$$= 40k\omega$$

$$T = 0.693RC$$

$$C = \frac{T}{0.693R}$$

$$= \frac{3 \times 10^{-3}}{0.693 \times 40 \times 10^3}$$

$$= 0.108\mu f$$

$$V_{b1} = -V_{bb}\frac{R_1}{R_1 + R_2} + V_{ce}\frac{R_2}{R_1 + R_2}$$

$$-1 = -V_{bb}\frac{R_1}{R_1 + R_1} \tag{3.8}$$

$$= \frac{-V_{bb}}{2}$$

$$V_{bb} = 2V$$

During Quasi stable state:

$$I_b(actual) = 0.15mA$$

$$I_{c1} = 2mA$$

$$I_4 = \frac{V_{cc} - V_{be}}{R_c + R - 1}$$

$$\frac{6}{3 + R_1}$$

$$I_5 = \frac{V_{be} - (-Vbb)}{R_2} \tag{3.9}$$

$$= \frac{2}{R_2}$$

$$I_b(actual) = I_4 - I_5$$

$$R_1 = R_2 = 21.8k\Omega$$

3.3 Astable Multivibrator

It has two quasi stable states. So no trigerring signal is required. It is also called as Free running multivibrator. The circuit diagram is shown in the figure 3.7 Assuming transistor T_1 is OFF and transistor T_2 is ON. During this state capacitor $C2$ charges through V_{CC}, R_2, T_2ON, capacitor $C1$ discharges through V_{CC}, R_C, T_2ON. When the voltage at base of transistor T_1 reaches the cut in voltage i.e V_{BE}, then the transistor T_1 is ON and transistor T_2 is OFF. This is first Quasi stable state.

During this state capacitor $C1$ charges through V_{CC}, R_1, T_1ON, capacitor $C2$ discharges through V_{CC}, R_C, T_1ON. When the voltage at base of transistor T_2 reaches the cut in voltage i.e V_{BE}, then the transistor T_1 is OFF and transistor T_2 is ON. This is second Quasi stable state. The output waveform at any collector terminal is a pure square wave signal. Because of this, astable multivibrator is called as Free running multivibrator.

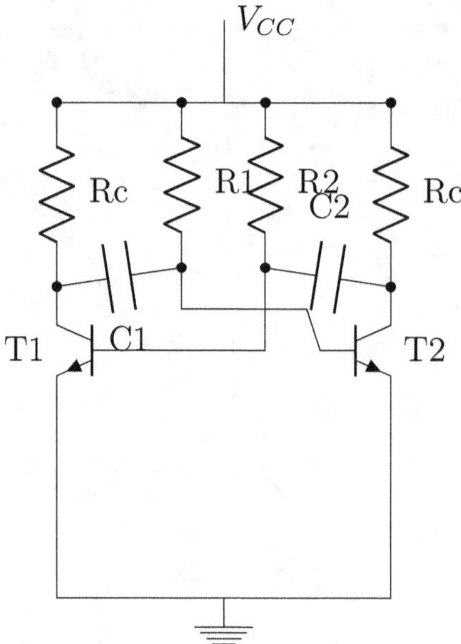

Figure 3.7: Collector Coupled Astable Multivibrator

3.3.1   Expression for Gate width

Consider the waveforms shown in the figure 3.8 for calculating gate width.
For first quasi stable state, Cosidering the expression

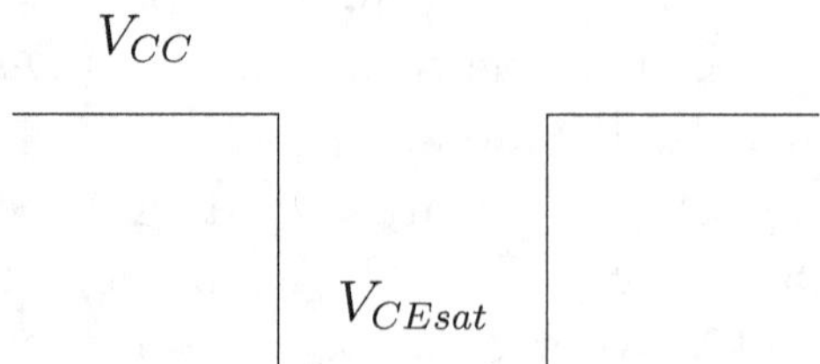

Figure 3.8: Output waveform of Astable multivibrator

$$V_o = V_f + (V_i - V_f)e^{\frac{-t_1}{R_1 C_1}}$$

$$V_{BE_{sat}} = V_{CC} + (-V_{CC} - V_{CC})e^{\frac{-t_1}{R_1 C_1}}$$

$$0 = V_{CC} - 2V_{CC}e^{\frac{-t_1}{R_1 C_1}}$$

$$\frac{1}{2} = e^{\frac{-t_1}{R_1 C_1}} \tag{3.10}$$

$$\ln(0.5) = \frac{-t_1}{R_1 C_1}$$

$$\boxed{t_1 = 0.69 R_1 C_1}$$

For second quasi stable state, Cosidering the expression

$$V_o = V_f + (V_i - V_f)e^{\frac{-t_2}{R_2 C_2}}$$

$$V_{BE_{sat}} = V_{CC} + (-V_{CC} - V_{CC})e^{\frac{-t_2}{R_2 C_2}}$$

$$0 = V_{CC} - 2V_{CC}e^{\frac{-t_2}{R_2 C_2}}$$

$$\frac{1}{2} = e^{\frac{-t_2}{R_2 C_2}} \tag{3.11}$$

$$\ln(0.5) = \frac{-t_2}{R_2 C_2}$$

$$\boxed{t_2 = 0.69 R_2 C_2}$$

Total gate width is given as

$$T = t_1 + t_2$$
$$= 0.69 R_1 C_1 + 0.69 R_2 C_2 \tag{3.12}$$

Assuming $R_1 = R_2 = R$ and $C_1 = C_2 = C$

$$\boxed{T = 1.38 RC} \tag{3.13}$$

3.3.2 Application of Astable multivibrator as Voltage to Frequency Converter

The very improtant application of Astable multivibrator is Voltage to Frequency Converter. The modified circuit diagram is shown in the figure 3.9 where by changing the voltage, frequency varies. So a variable voltage is introduced in the circuit diagram.

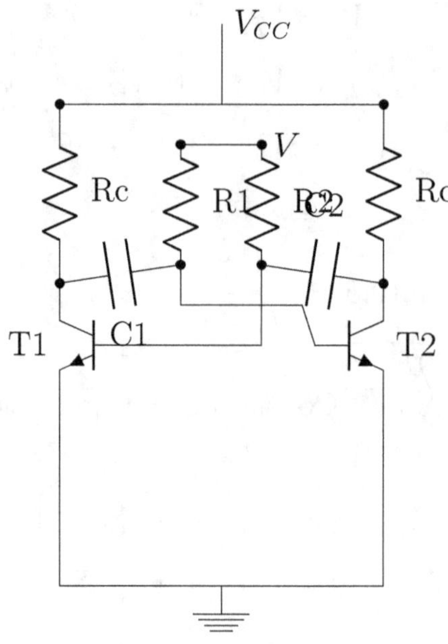

Figure 3.9: Application of Astable Multivibrator

$$V_o = V_f + (V_i - V_f)e^{\frac{-t_1}{R_1 C_1}}$$

$$V_{BE_{sat}} = V + (-V_{CC} - V)e^{\frac{-t_1}{R_1 C_1}}$$

$$0 = V - (V_{CC} + V)e^{\frac{-t_1}{R_1 C_1}}$$

$$(V_{CC} + V)e^{\frac{-t_1}{R_1 C_1}} = V \tag{3.14}$$

$$e^{\frac{-t_1}{R_1 C_1}} = \frac{V}{(V_{CC} + V)}$$

$$\boxed{t_1 = R_1 C_1 \ln[1 + \frac{V_{CC}}{V}]}$$

Similarly

$$\boxed{t_2 = R_2 C_2 \ln[1 + \frac{V_{CC}}{V}]} \tag{3.15}$$

Total gate width is given as $T = T_1 + T_2$ and also assuming $R_1 = R_2 = R$ and $C_1 = C_2 = C$

$$\boxed{T = 2RC \ln[1 + \frac{V_{CC}}{V}]} \tag{3.16}$$

Frequency is given as

$$F = \frac{1}{2RC\ln[1 + \frac{V_{CC}}{V}]} \tag{3.17}$$

3.3.3 Problems

1. For astable multivibrator if $R_1 = 20K\Omega, R_2 = 10K\Omega, C_1 = 0.02\mu f$, $C_1 = 0.05\mu f$. Find frequency of oscillations and duty cycle.

   Solution

   From the equations
   $$\begin{aligned} T_1 &= 0.69R_1C_1 \\ &= 0.27msec \\ T_2 &= 0.69R_2C_2 \\ &= 0.1035msec \\ T &= T_1 + T_2 \\ &= 0.37535msec \\ F &= \frac{1}{T} \\ &= 2.67KHz \end{aligned} \tag{3.18}$$

   Duty cycle is given as
   $$\begin{aligned} DC &= \frac{T_1}{T_1 + T_2} \\ &= 0.72 \end{aligned} \tag{3.19}$$

2. Find the period of output and frequency of oscillations of an astable multivibrator with $R_1 = R_2 = K\Omega$ and $C_1 = C_2 = \mu f$

   Solution

   From the expression derived earlier,
   $$\begin{aligned} T &= 1.38RC \\ &= 1.38 \times 25 \times 10^3 \times 0.2 \times 10^{-6} \\ T &= 6.9msec \\ F &= 144.9Hz \end{aligned} \tag{3.20}$$

3. Find the ratio $\frac{V_{CC}}{V}$ if a voltage to frequency converter generates oscillations of frequency twice of that when $V = V_{CC}$.

Solution

From the given problem assume

$$F_2 = \frac{1}{2RC\ln[1 + \frac{V_{CC}}{V}]} \tag{3.21}$$

if a voltage to frequency converter generates oscillations of frequency twice of that when $V = V_{CC}$, then

$$F_1 = \frac{1}{2RC\ln[1 + \frac{V_{CC}}{V_{CC}}]}$$
$$= \frac{1}{2RC\ln(2)} \tag{3.22}$$

As per the problem,$F_2 = 2 \times F_1$ Substituting the equations of F_2 and F_1.

$$\frac{1}{2RC\ln[1 + \frac{V_{CC}}{V}]} = 2 \times \frac{1}{2RC\ln(2)}$$

$$\ln(2) = 2 \times \ln[1 + \frac{V_{CC}}{V}] \tag{3.23}$$

$$\frac{V_{CC}}{V} = 0.411$$

4. Design an astable multivibrator to generate a square wave of 1KHz.

Solution

Assuming the square wave is symmetrical and also considering the design steps of multivibrators for the circuit diagram shown in the figure 3.10 Assumptions:

$I_c sat = 5mA$, $V_{CC} = 12V$, $hfe = 25$

Calculating the values of resistors and capacitors:

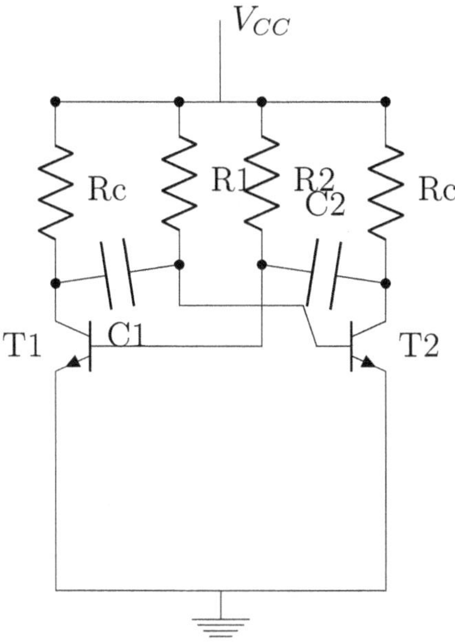

Figure 3.10: Problem 3 : Astable Multivibrator

$$
\begin{aligned}
R_C &= \frac{V_{CC} - V_{CE}}{I_C} \\
&= \frac{12 - 0.2}{5m} \\
&= 2.36K\Omega \\
I_b &= \frac{I_C}{hfe} \\
&= 0.2mA \\
I_{B_{actual}} &= 1.5 \times I_B \\
&= 0.3mA \\
R_1 &= \frac{V_{CC} - V_{BE}}{I_{B_{actual}}} \\
&= \frac{12 - 0.6}{0.3m} \\
&= 38K\Omega
\end{aligned}
\tag{3.24}
$$

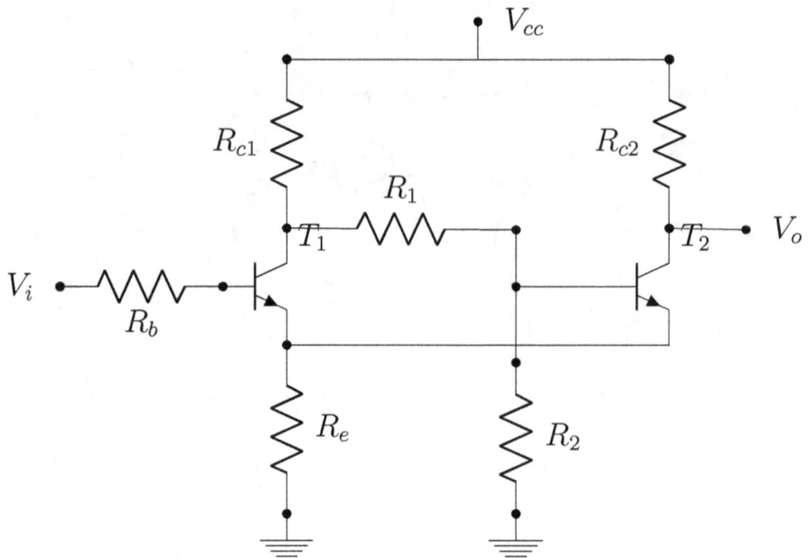

Figure 3.11: Schmitt Trigger

As the time period is given as

$$T = 1.38RC$$

$$C = \frac{T}{1.38R}$$

$$= 0.01\mu f$$

(3.25)

3.4   Schmitt Trigger

Schmitt trigger is a type of bistable multivibrator. It has only one DC coupling. It is used to generate a square wave from sine wave. Both the collectors are connected to supply voltage V_{cc} through resistors. The emitters of both the transistors are connected to negative supply through common resistor. Input signal is applied to base of transistor T_1. The collector of transistor T_1 is connected to base of transistor T_2 through resistor which is shown in the figure 3.12

Let the input signal $V_i = V_m sin\omega t$. When $V_i = 0$, transistor T_1 is OFF but the transistor T_2 will be in active region as the collector voltage of transistor T_1 is approximately equal to V_{cc}. Let I_{c2} is the collector current and I_{e2} is the emitter current of transistor T_2. The voltage drop across the resistor R_e is $I_{e2}R_e$. If $I_{c2} = I_{e2}$, then $V_e = I_{c2}R_e$. As long as $v_i < V_e + V_\gamma$, T_1 will

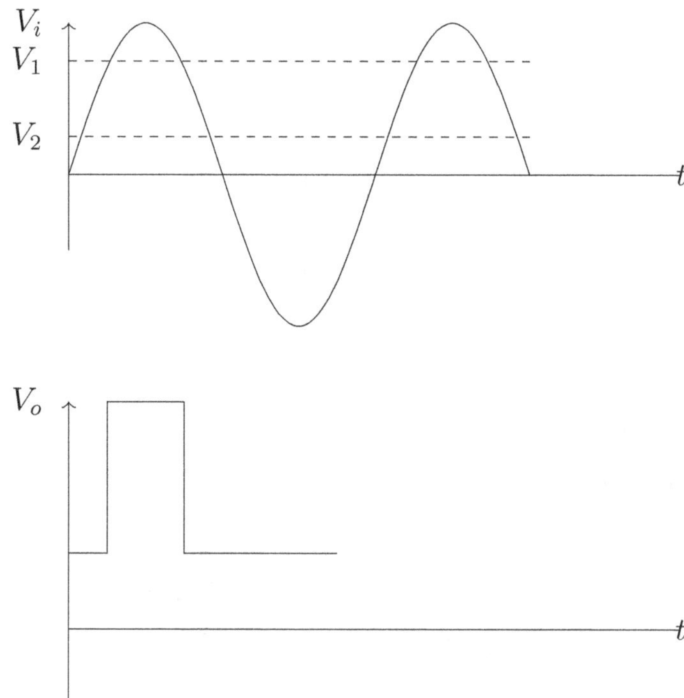

Figure 3.12: Output waveforms of Schmitt trigger circuit

remain in OFF.When a positive voltage is applied to base of transistor T_1, transistor T_1 will ON which makes transistor T_2 to OFF. This value of input voltage which makes transistor T_1 ON is called as Upper Trigger Point UTP which is represented as V_{UTP} and expressed as $V_{UTP} = I_{c2}R_+V_\gamma$.

As input voltage V_i decreases, the transistor T_2 will ON and transistor T_1 is OFF. This value of input voltage which makes transistor T_2 ON is called as Lower Trigger Point LTP which is represented as V_{LTP} and expressed as $V_{LTP} = V_{be}act + I_{c1}R_e$. The input and output wave forms are shown in the figure 3.12

Hysteresis Loop

The output voltage from V_{cc} to $V_{cc} - I_cR_c$ i.e from high to low and from $V_{cc} - I_cR_c$ to V_{cc} occurs at different points. This is known as Hystersis loop. The Hysteresis loop is shown in the figure 3.13

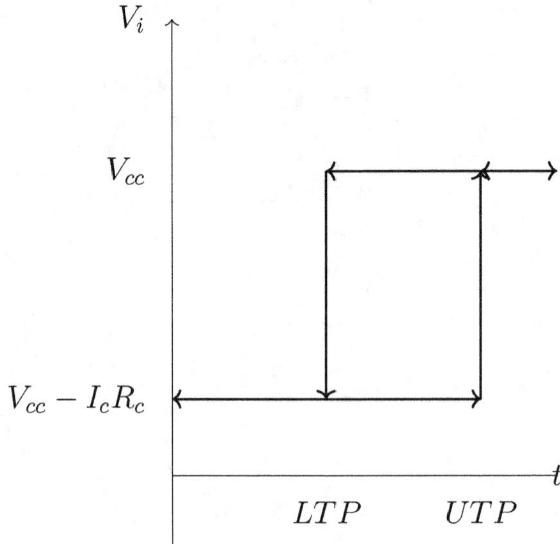

Figure 3.13: Hysteresis Loop

Expression of UTP

To derive the expression for UTP, applying Thevenin's equivalent to transistor T_2 and calculating Thevenin's voltage V' and Thevenin's Resistance R' is shwon in the figure 3.14.

$$V' = \frac{V_{cc}R_2}{R_{c1} + R_1 + R_2}$$

$$R' = \frac{R_2(R_{c1} + R_1)}{R_{c1} + R_1 + R_2}$$

$$(3.26)$$

Let assume the transistor T_2 is in active region, then

$$-i_{e2} = i_{c2} + i_{b2}$$

$$i_{c2} = h_{fe}I_{b2}$$

$$-i_{e2} = i_{c2} + i_{b2}$$

$$= (h_{fe} + 1)i_{b2}$$

$$(3.27)$$

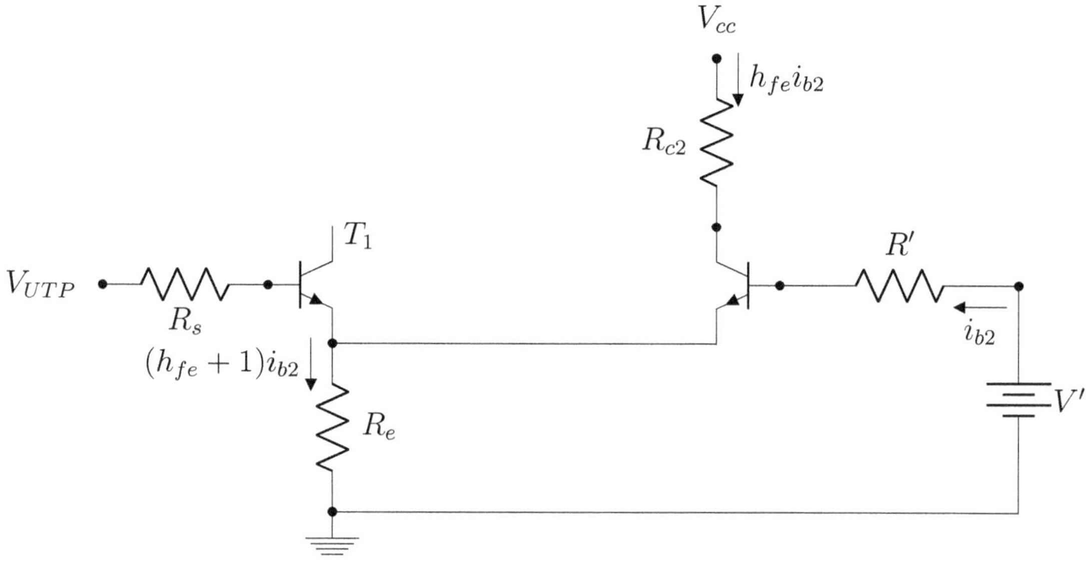

Figure 3.14: Schmitt Trigger Circuit when T_1 is just ON

Applying KVL around base of the transistor T_2,

$$V' - V_{be2} = (R' + R_e(h_{fe} + 1))i_{b2}$$

$$i_{b2} = \frac{V' - V_{be2}}{(R' + R_e(h_{fe} + 1))}$$

$$V_e = (i_{c2} + i_{b2})R_e$$

$$= (h_{fe} + 1)i_{b2}R_e$$

$$= (V' - V_{be2})\frac{R_e(h_{fe} + 1)}{R' + R_e(h_{fe} + 1)} \tag{3.28}$$

$$V_{UTP} = V_e + V_{\gamma 1}$$

$$V_{UTP} \approx V' - V_{be2} + V_{\gamma 1}$$

$$\approx V' - 0.1$$

Expression for LTP

To derive the expression for UTP, applying Thevenin's equivalent to transistor T_1 and calculating Thevenin's voltage V'' and Thevenin's Resistance R''

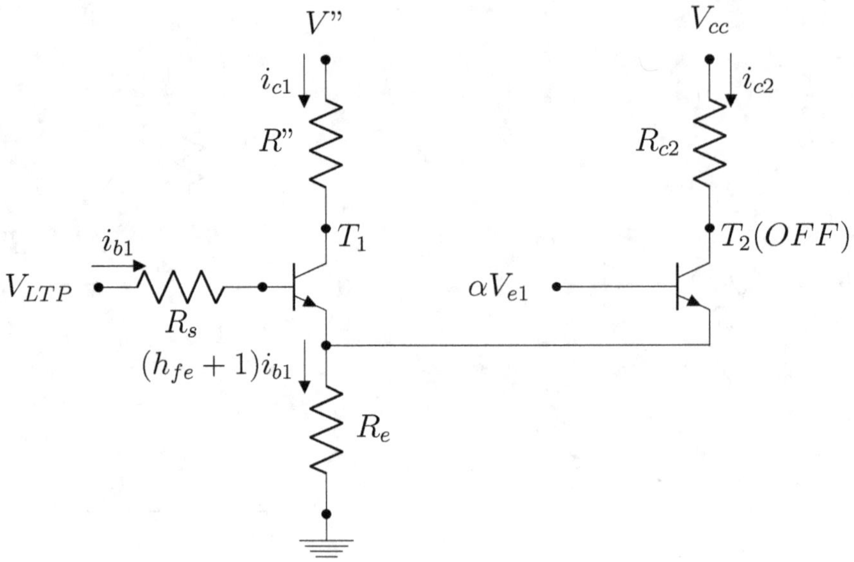

Figure 3.15: Schmitt Trigger Circuit when T_1 is OFF

for the circuit shown in the figure 3.15.

$$V'' = \frac{V_{cc}(R_1 + R_2)}{R_{c1} + R_1 + R_2}$$

$$R'' = \frac{R_{c1}(R_2 R_1)}{R_{c1} + R_1 + R_2}$$

$$\alpha = \frac{R_2}{R_1 + R_2} \tag{3.29}$$

$$V' = \alpha V''$$

$$-i_{e1} = i_{b1} + i_{c1}$$

$$V_e = -i_{e1} R_e$$

$$= (i_{b1} + i_{c1}) R_e$$

Applying KVL around base of the transistor T_2,

$$-\alpha V_{cn1} + V_{\gamma 2} + V_e = 0$$

$$-\alpha V_{cn1} + V_{\gamma 2} + (i_{b1} + i_{c1})R_e = 0$$

$$V_{cn1} = V" - i_{c1}R"$$

$$i_{c1} = h_{fe}ib1$$

$$= \frac{\alpha V" - V_{\gamma 2}}{\alpha R" + R'_e}$$

$$= \frac{V' - V_{\gamma 2}}{\alpha R" + R'_e}$$

$$R'_e = R_e[1 + \frac{1}{h_{fe}}]$$

$$V_{LTP} = i_{b1}R_s + V_{be1} + V_e$$

$$= i_{b1}R_s + V_{be1} + (i_{c1} + ib1)R_e$$

$$= \frac{i_{c1}R_s}{h_{hfe}} + V_{be1} + i_{c1}R_e[1 + \frac{1}{h_{fe}}]$$

$$= V_{be1} + i_{c1}[R'_e + \frac{R_s}{h_{fe}}]$$

$$= V_{be1} + \frac{R'_e + \frac{R_s}{h_{fe}}}{\alpha R" + R'_e}(V' - V_{\gamma 2})$$

$$= V_{be1} + \frac{R_e}{\alpha R + R_e}(V' - V_{\gamma 2})$$

$$(3.30)$$

Problem

Design a Schmitt trigger circuit to have V_{cc}=12V, UTP=6V,LTP=3V. Assume npn transistors with $h_{ffe}min$=60.

Solution The circuit is shown in the figure 3.16. Given parameters V_{cc}=12V, UTP=6V,LTP=3V, $h_{ffe}min$=60. Assume i_{c2}=2mA, i_2=0.2mA.

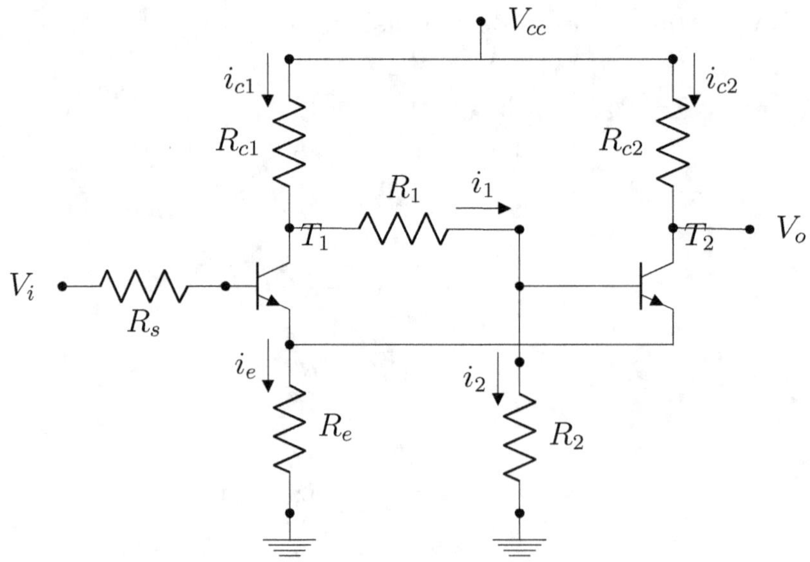

Figure 3.16: Schmitt Trigger Circuit to be designed

$$UTP = V_1$$
$$= V_e + V_{\gamma 1}$$
$$V_e = V_1 - V_{\gamma 1}$$
$$= 6 - 0.5$$
$$= 5.5V$$
$$R_e = \frac{V_e}{i_{e2}}$$
$$= \frac{5.5}{2 \times 10^{-3}}$$
$$= 2.75k\Omega$$
$$R_s << h_{fe}R_e \qquad (3.31)$$
$$R_s << 60 \times 2.75 = 165k\Omega$$
$$R_s = 2k\Omega$$
$$V_{ce}active = \frac{1}{3}V_{cc}$$
$$= 4V$$
$$V_{cc} - i_{c2}R_{c2} - V_{ce}active - i_{c2}R_e = 0$$
$$R_{c2} = \frac{V_{cc} - V_{ce}active - i_{c2}R_e}{i_{c2}}$$
$$= \frac{12 - 4 - 5.5}{2}$$
$$= 1.25k\Omega$$

$$\begin{aligned}
R_2 &= \frac{V_{b2}}{i_2} \\
&= \frac{V_e + V_{be2}}{0.2} \\
&= \frac{6.2}{0.2} \\
&= 31k\Omega
\end{aligned} \tag{3.32}$$

$$\begin{aligned}
i_{b2} &= \frac{i_{c2}}{h_{fe}} \\
&= \frac{2 \times 10^{-3}}{60} \\
&= 33.3\mu A \\
i_1 &= \frac{V_{cc} - V_{b2}}{R_{c1} + R_1} \\
i_1 &== i_2 + i_{b2} \\
&= 0.23mA
\end{aligned} \tag{3.33}$$

$$\begin{aligned}
R_{c1} + R_1 &= 24.89k\Omega \\
LTP &= V_2 \\
&= V_{be1} + \frac{R_e}{\alpha R + R_e}(V' - V_{\gamma 2}) \\
V' &= V_1 + 0.1 \\
R &= 4.93k\Omega \\
R_{c1} &= 5.4k\Omega \\
R_1 &= 19.4k\Omega
\end{aligned}$$

3.5   Triggering

It is a process of applying an additional signal to change the output from one state to other. There are two types of triggering.

1. Unsymmetrical Triggering: It uses two sources.

2. Symmetrical Triggering: It uses only one source.

Chapter 4

Realization of Logic gates

Logic gates are essential in designing a digital circuit. Each logic gate have one or more inputs and only one input. The relation between input and output is based on a particular logic. Different logic gates are NOT,AND,OR which are basic gates and NAND and NOR which are universal gates.

In this chapter we will design logic gates using different logic families like using Diodes, Transistors,DTL,RTL,TTL,ECL.

4.1 NOT gate or Inverter

The logic diagram of NOT is shown in the figure 4.1 Truth table of NOT gate is given in the table 4.1

4.2 AND gate

The logic diagram and boolean expression of AND gate is shown in the figure 4.2 The truth table of AND gate is given in the table 4.2

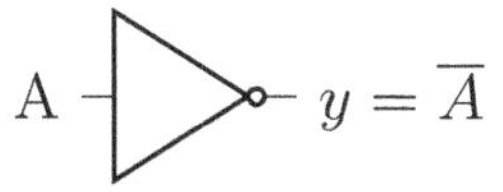

$$A \longrightarrow y = \overline{A}$$

Figure 4.1: NOT gate

A	$y = \overline{A}$
0	1
1	0

Table 4.1: NOT gate Truth table

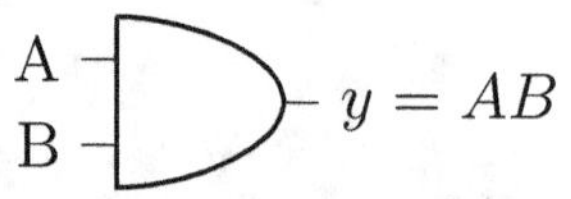

$$y = AB$$

Figure 4.2: AND gate

A	B	$y = AB$
0	0	0
0	1	0
1	0	0
1	1	1

Table 4.2: AND gate Truth table

4.3   OR gate

The logic diagram and boolean expression of OR gate is shown in the figure 4.3 The truth table of OR gate is given in the table 4.3

A	B	$y = A + B$
0	0	0
0	1	1
1	0	1
1	1	1

Table 4.3: OR gate Truth table

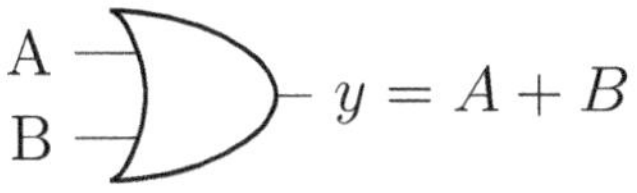

Figure 4.3: OR gate

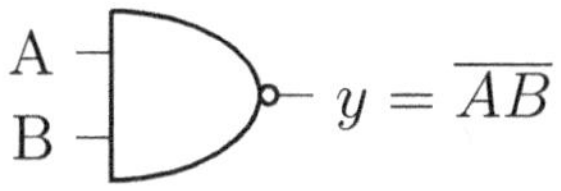

Figure 4.4: NAND gate

4.4 NAND gate

The logic diagram and boolean expression of NAND gate is shown in the figure 4.4 The truth table of NAND gate is given in the table 4.4

A	B	$y = \overline{AB}$
0	0	1
0	1	1
1	0	1
1	1	0

Table 4.4: NAND gate ruth table

4.5 NOR gate

The logic diagram and boolean expression of NOR gate is shown in the figure 4.5 The truth table of NOR gate is given in the table4.5

4.6 Two input AND gate using Diodes

The circuit diagram of two input AND gate using Diodes is shown in the figure 4.6

Working

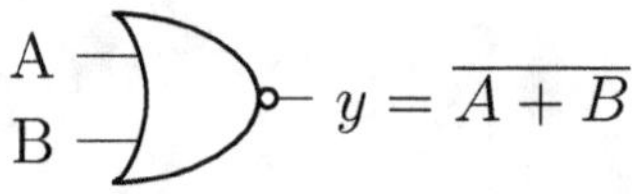

$$A \quad B \quad y = \overline{A + B}$$

Figure 4.5: NOR gate

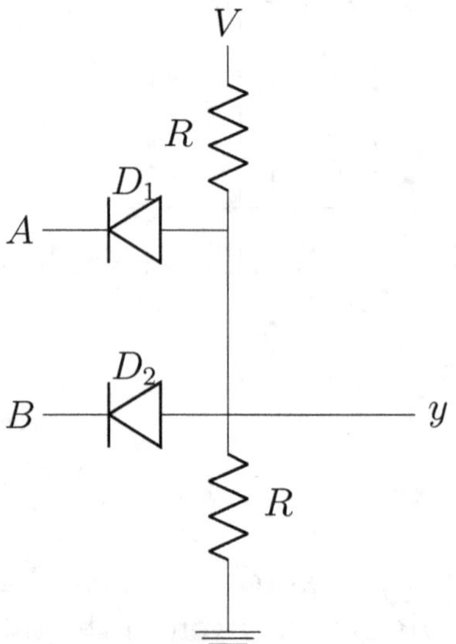

Figure 4.6: Two input AND gate using Diodes

A	B	$y = \overline{A + B}$
0	0	1
0	1	0
1	0	0
1	1	0

Table 4.5: NOR gate truth table

The working of two input AND gate using Diodes is shown in the following table 4.6

A	B	D_1	D_2	$y = AB$
0	0	ON	ON	0
0	1	ON	OFF	0
1	0	OFF	ON	0
1	1	OFF	OFF	1

Table 4.6: Two input AND gate using Diodes Truth table

4.7 Two input OR gate using Diodes

The circuit diagram of two input OR gate using Diodes is shown in the figure 4.7

Working

The working of two input OR gate using Diodes is shown in the following table 4.7

A	B	D_1	D_2	$y = A + B$
0	0	OFF	OFF	0
0	1	OFF	ON	1
1	0	ON	OFF	1
1	1	ON	ON	1

Table 4.7: Two input OR gate using Diodes Table

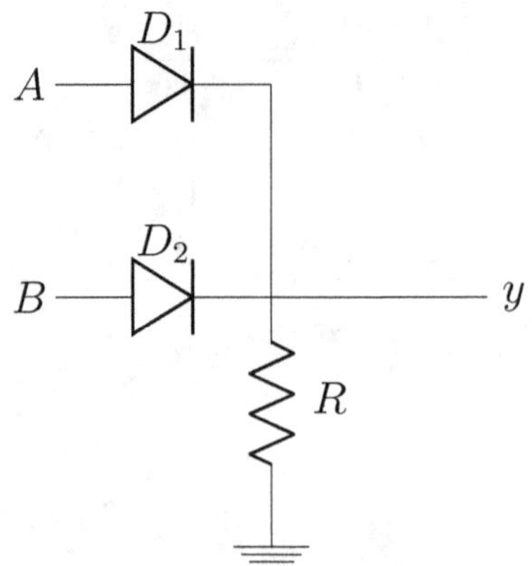

Figure 4.7: Two input OR gate using Diodes

4.8   NOT gate using Transistor

The circuit diagram of NOT gate using Transistor is shown in the figure 4.8
The working of NOT gate using Transistor is shown in the following table
4.8

A	T	$y = \overline{A}$
0	Cut off	1
1	Saturation	0

Table 4.8: NOT gate using Transistor table

4.9   Two input NAND gate using transistors

The circuit diagram of Two input NAND gate using transistors is shown in
the figure 4.9

   The working of two input NAND gate using transistors is given in the
following table 4.9

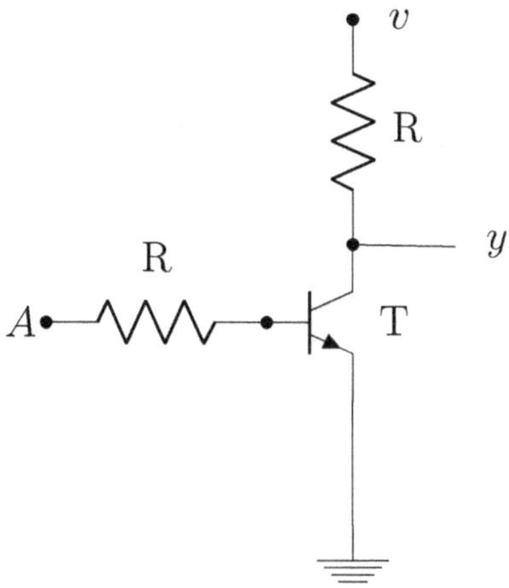

Figure 4.8: NOT gate using Transistor

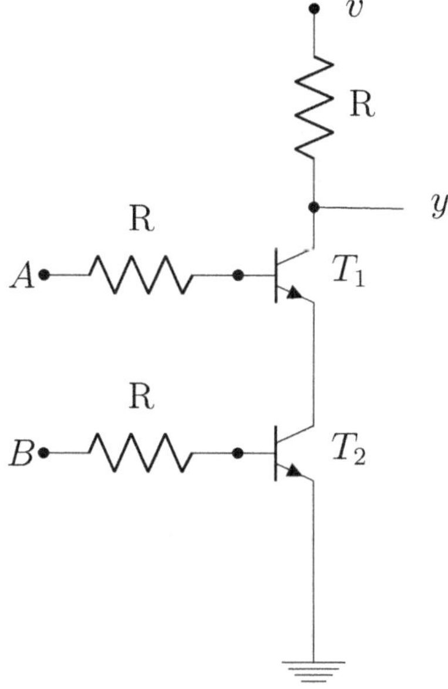

Figure 4.9: Two input NAND gate using transistors

A	B	T_1	T_2	$y = \overline{AB}$
0	0	Cut off	Cut off	1
0	1	Cut off	Saturation	1
1	0	Saturation	Cut off	1
1	1	Saturation	Saturation	0

Table 4.9: Two input NAND gate using transistors table

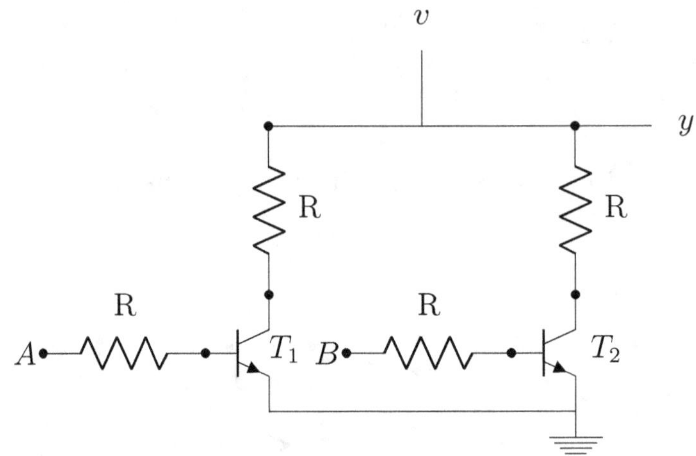

Figure 4.10: Two input NOR gate using Transistors

4.10 Two input NOR gate using Transistors

The circuit diagram of Two input NOR gate using Transistors is shown in the figure 4.10 The working of Two input NOR gate using Transistors is shown in the following table 4.10

4.11 NOT gate using DTL

The circuit diagram of NOT gate using DTL is shown in the figure 4.11 The working of NOT gate using Transistor is shown in the following table 4.11

A	B	T_1	T_2	$y = \overline{A + B}$
0	0	Cut off	Cut off	1
0	1	Cut off	Saturation	0
1	0	Saturation	Cut off	0
1	1	Saturation	Saturation	0

Table 4.10: Two input NOR gate using Transistors table

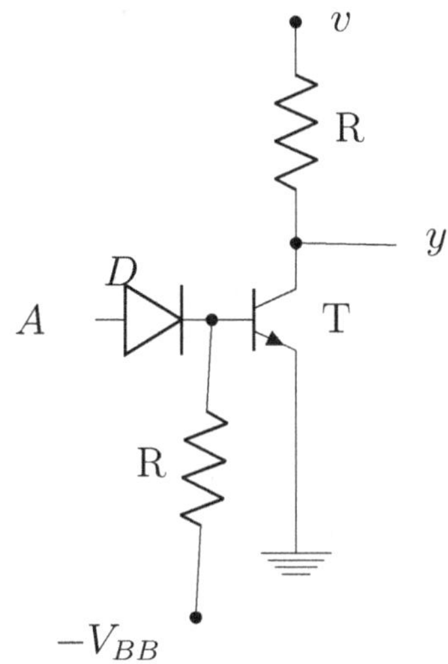

Figure 4.11: NOT gate using DTL

A	D	T	$y = \overline{A}$
0	ON	Cut off	1
1	OFF	Saturation	0

Table 4.11: NOT gate using DTL table

4.12 NAND gate using DTL

The circuit diagram of NAND gate using DTL is shown in the figure 4.12
The working of NAND gate using DTL circuit diagram is shown in the below
table 4.12

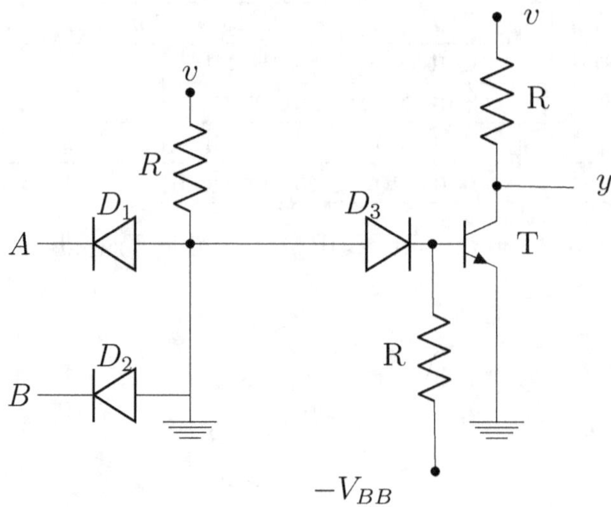

Figure 4.12: NAND gate using DTL

A	B	D_1	D_2	D_3	T	$y = \overline{AB}$
0	0	ON	ON	OFF	Cut off	1
0	1	ON	OFF	OFF	Cut off	0
1	0	OFF	ON	OFF	Cut off	1
1	1	OFF	OFF	ON	Saturation	0

Table 4.12: NAND gate using DTL truth table

4.13　NOR gate using DTL

The circuit diagram of NOR gate using DTL is shown in the figure 4.13 The working of NOR gate using DTL circuit diagram is shown in the below table 4.13

4.14　Emitter Coupled OR/NOR gate

The Emitter Coupled OR/NOR gate circuit diagram is shown in the figure 4.14 The working of Emitter Coupled OR/NOR gate using Diodes and Transistors is shown in the following table 4.14

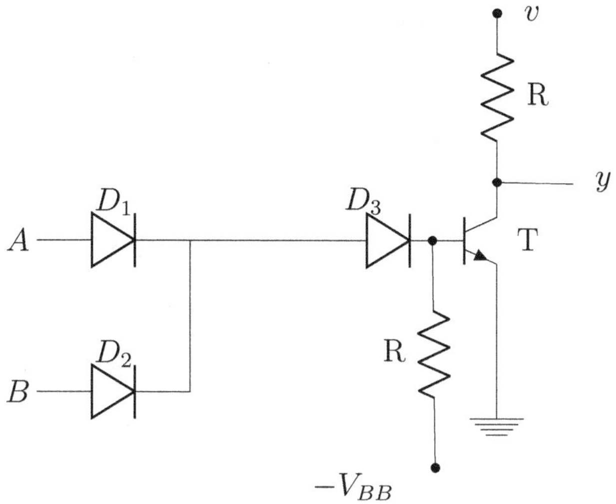

Figure 4.13: NOR gate using DTL

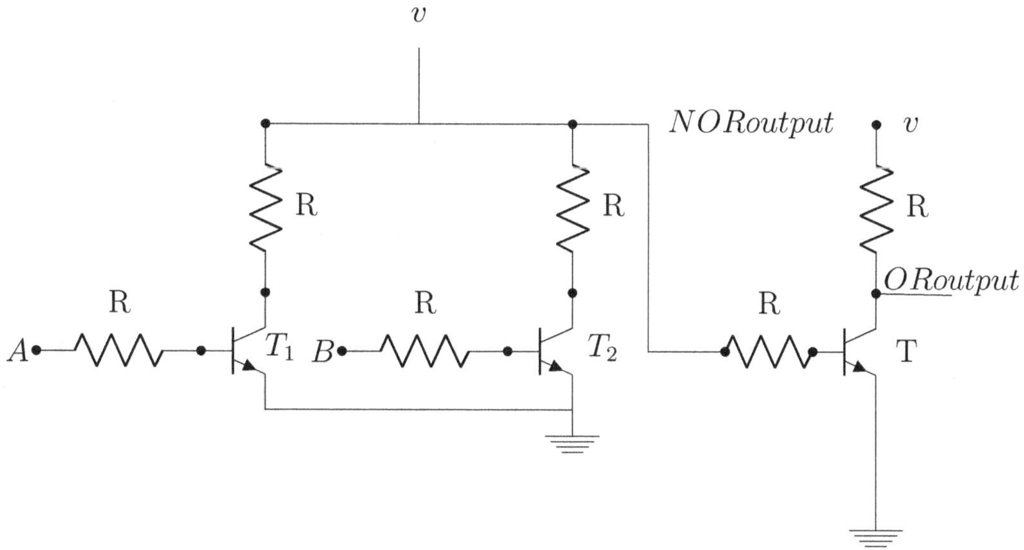

Figure 4.14: Emitter Coupled OR/NOR gate

A	B	D_1	D_2	D_3	T	$y = \overline{A+B}$
0	0	OFF	OFF	ON	Cut off	1
0	1	OFF	ON	ON	Saturation	0
1	0	ON	OFF	ON	Saturation	0
1	1	ON	ON	ON	Saturation	0

Table 4.13: NOR gate using DTL truth table

A	B	T_1	T_2	NOR output	T_3	OR output
0	0	Cut off	Cut off	1	Saturation	0
0	1	Cut off	Saturation	0	Cut off	1
1	0	Saturation	Cut off	0	Cut off	1
1	1	Saturation	Saturation	0	Cut off	1

Table 4.14: Emitter Coupled OR/NOR gate truth table

4.15   TTL NAND gate

The circuit diagram of TTL NAND gate is shown in the figure 4.15 The transistor T is a multi emitter npn. To analyze the circuit diagram, multi emitter transistor is replaced with the diodes which is shown in the circuit diagram 4.16

The working of TTL NAND gate is expalined in the following table 4.15

A	B	D_1	D_2	D_3	T_1	T_2	T_3	D_4	$y = \overline{AB}$
0	0	ON	ON	OFF	Cut off	Cut off	Saturation	ON	1
0	1	ON	OFF	OFF	Cut off	Cut off	Saturation	ON	1
1	0	OFF	ON	OFF	Cut off	Cut off	Saturation	ON	1
1	1	OFF	OFF	ON	Saturation	Saturation	Cut off	OFF	0

Table 4.15: TTL NAND GATE truth table

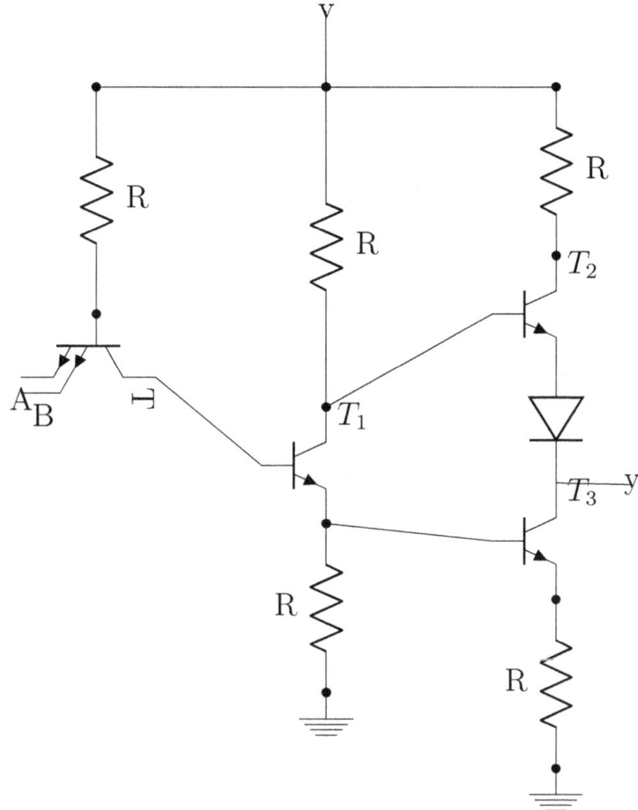

Figure 4.15: TTL NAND gate

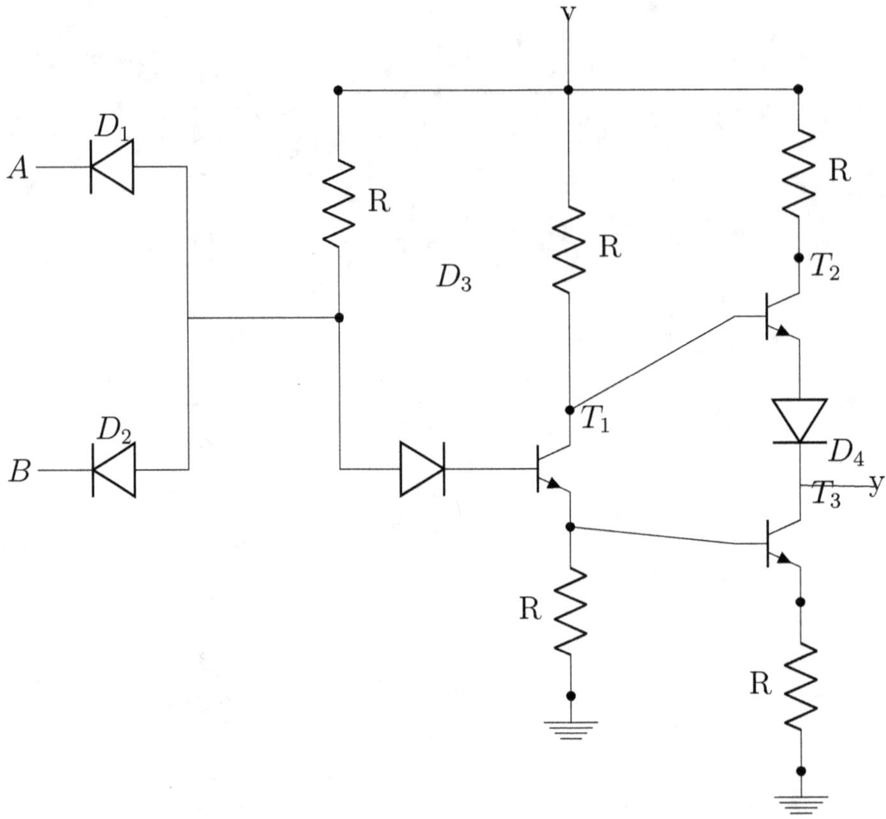

Figure 4.16: TTL NAND gate using diodes

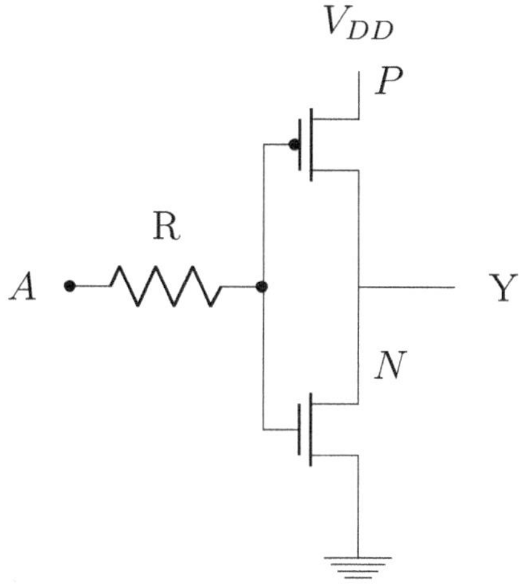

Figure 4.17: CMOS NOT gate

4.16 CMOS NOT gate

The circuit diagram of CMOS NOT gate is shown in the figure 4.17 The
working of CMOS NOT gate is explained in the following table 4.16

A	PMOS	NMOS	Y
0	ON	OFF	1
1	OFF	ON	0

Table 4.16: CMOS NOT gate truth table

4.17 Two input CMOS NAND gate

The circuit diagram of Two input CMOS NAND gate is shown in the figure
4.18 The working of CMOS NAND gate is explained in the following table
4.17

4.18 CMOS NOR gate

The circuit diagram of CMOS NOR gate is shown in the figure 4.19 The

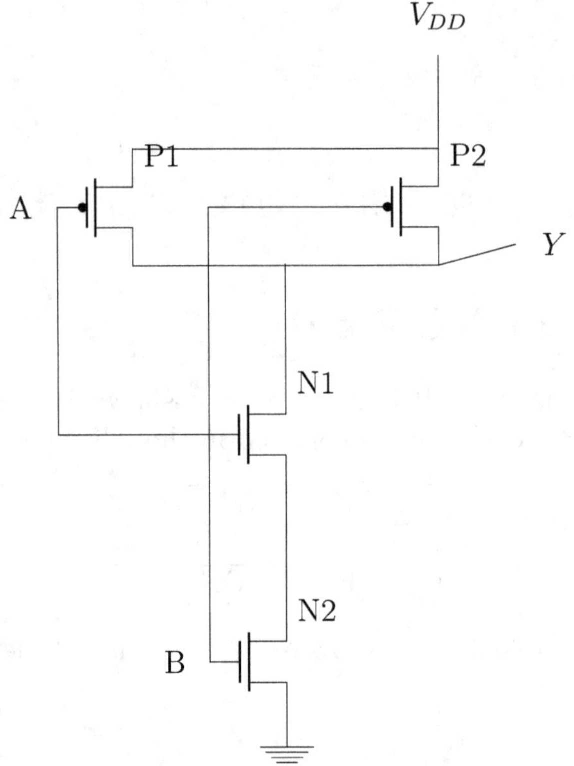

Figure 4.18: CMOS NAND gate

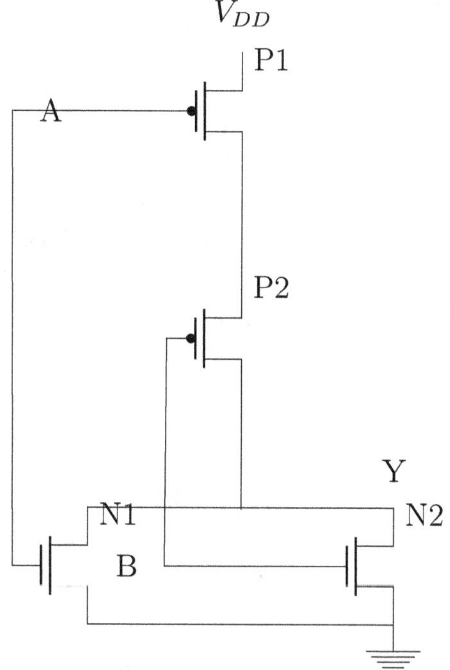

Figure 4.19: CMOS NOR gate

A	B	P1	P2	N1	N2	Y
0	0	ON	ON	OFF	OFF	1
0	1	ON	OFF	OFF	ON	1
1	0	OFF	ON	ON	OFF	1
1	1	OFF	OFF	ON	ON	0

Table 4.17: CMOS NAND gate truth table

working of CMOS NOR gate is explained in the following table 4.18

A	B	P1	P2	N1	N2	Y
0	0	ON	ON	OFF	OFF	1
0	1	ON	OFF	OFF	ON	0
1	0	OFF	ON	ON	OFF	0
1	1	OFF	OFF	ON	ON	1

Table 4.18: CMOS NOR gate table

4.19   Comparision of Logic families

The differences between different logic families is shown in the following table 4.19

Parameter	DTL	TTL	ECL	CMOS
Basic Gates	NAND	NAND	OR/NOR	NAND/NOR
Fan Out	8	10	25	>50
Propagation Delay (nanosec)	1.5-3.3	1.5 - 3.3	1-4	1-200
Clock Frequency(MHz)	72	35	>60	10
Power Dissipation(mwatts)	8-12	10	40-55	0.0025

Table 4.19: Comparision of Logic families table

Chapter 5

Time Base Generators

Circuits which genertes linear sweep with respect to time are called as Time Base Generators. They are of two types:

1. Voltage Time Base Generators: The circuits which can generate voltage wrt to time are called **Voltage Time Base Generators**.

2. Current Time Base Generators: The circuits which can generate current wrt to time are called **CurrentTime Base Generators**.

The linear sweep waveform is shown in the figure 5.1a. The Exponential sweep waveform is shown in the figure 5.1b. Sweep time T_s is the time taken by the capacitor to charge and Return time T_r is the time taken by the capacitor to discharge and V_s is sweep voltage. The difference between linear sweep and exponential sweep is called an Error. There are three errors:

1. Slope or Sweep Speed error

2. Displacement error

3. Transmission error

5.1   Slope or Sweep Speed error e_s

The rate of change of voltage with respect to time is called as Sweep Speed. The error caused by sweep speed is called as **Slope or Sweep Speed error**. It is denoted as e_s and is given as

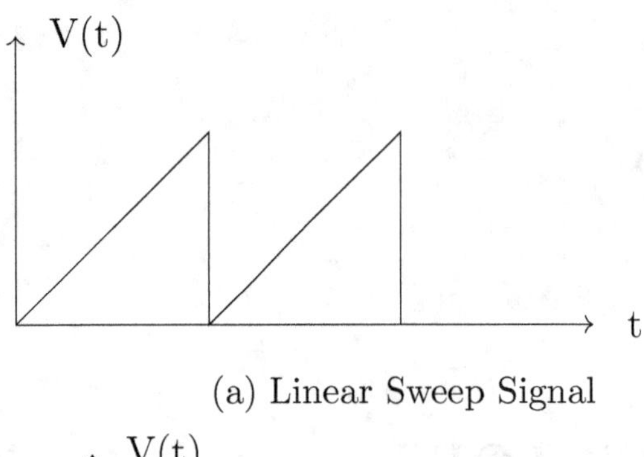

(a) Linear Sweep Signal

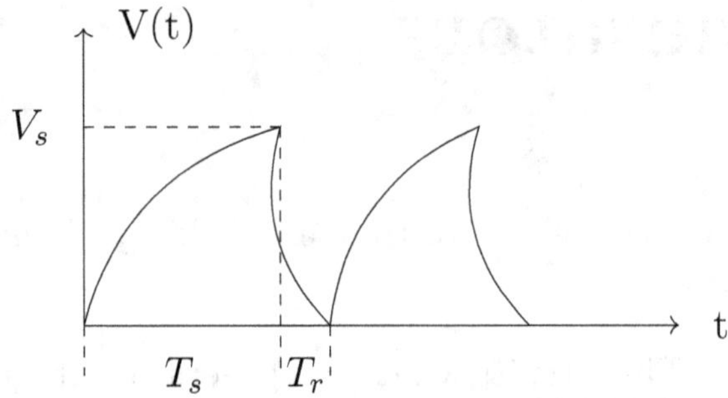

(b) Exponential Sweep Signal

$$e_s = \frac{\frac{dV_s}{dt}\big|_{t=0} - \frac{dV_s}{dt}\big|_{t=T_s}}{\frac{dV_s}{dt}\big|_{t=0}}$$

$$V_s = A(1 - e^{-t/RC})$$

(5.1)

Where A is the input voltage applied to RC circuit. Differentiating the V_s wrt time and submitting in the sweep speed error, we get

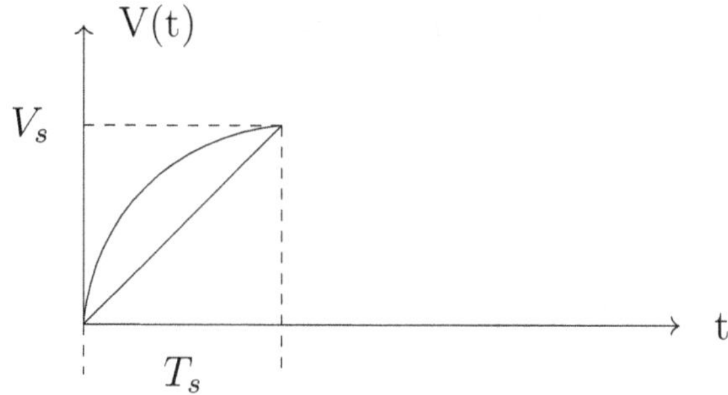

Figure 5.2: Dis[lacement Error

$$\frac{\mathrm{d}V_S}{\mathrm{d}t} = A(-e^{-t/RC}(-1/RC))$$

$$= A(\frac{e^{-t/RC}}{RC})$$

$$\frac{\mathrm{d}V_s}{\mathrm{d}t}\Big|_{t=0} = \frac{A}{RC}$$

$$\frac{\mathrm{d}V_s}{\mathrm{d}t}\Big|_{t=T_s} = \frac{Ae^{-T_s RC}}{RC}$$

$$e_s = \frac{\frac{A}{RC} - \frac{Ae^{-T_s/RC}}{RC}}{\frac{A}{RC}}$$

$$= 1 - e^{-T_s/RC}$$

(5.2)

Expanding the exponential term

$$\boxed{e_s = 1 - [1 - \frac{T_s}{RC}]}$$

(5.3)

5.2 Displacement Error e_d

It is defined as the ratio of maximum difference between generated and actual sweep with the amplitude of sweep at the end of sweep time. It is denoted as e_d and is shown in the figure 5.2

$$e_d = \frac{|V_s - V_s'|_{max}}{V_s'|_{t=T_s}}$$

(5.4)

V_s' is the linear sweep voltage. Submitting and expanding the term V_s and $V_s' = \alpha t$ in the expression. α is slope.

$$V_s = A[1 - e^{-t/RC}]$$

$$= a[1 - (1 - \frac{t}{RC} + \frac{t^2}{2R^2C^2})] \tag{5.5}$$

$$V_s = A[\frac{t}{RC} - \frac{t^2}{2R^2C^2}]$$

Let the maximum difference at $t = \frac{T_s}{2}$

$$V_s = A[\frac{T_s}{2RC} - \frac{T_s^2}{8R^2C^2}]$$

$$V_s' = \alpha t$$

$$\alpha = \frac{dV_s}{dt}\big|_{t=0}$$

$$= \frac{A}{RC}e^{-t/RC}\big|_{t=0} \tag{5.6}$$

$$\alpha = \frac{A}{RC}$$

$$V_s' = \frac{At}{RC}$$

$$= \frac{AT_s}{2RC}$$

$$\boxed{e_d = \frac{T_s}{8RC}} \tag{5.7}$$

5.3   Transmission Error e_t

When a ramp input signal is applied to high pass RC circuit, the output signal deviates from the expected signal which is shown in the figure 5.3

$$e_t = \frac{V_s' - V_s}{V_s'} \tag{5.8}$$

$$\boxed{e_t = \frac{T_s}{2RC}} \tag{5.9}$$

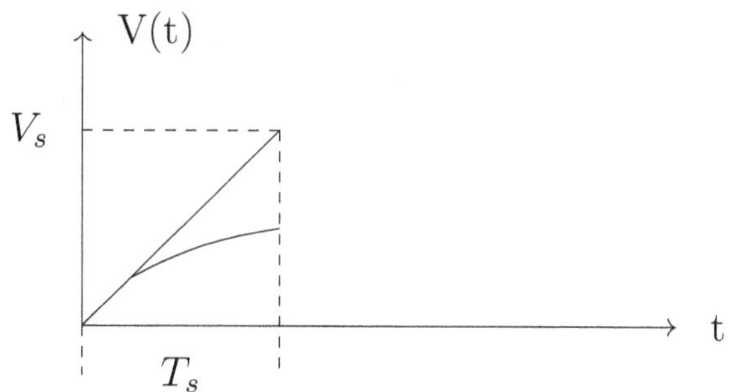

Figure 5.3: Transmission Error

5.4 Relation between e_s, e_d and e_t

The relation between e_s, e_d and e_t is given as

$$\boxed{e_d = \frac{e_s}{8} = \frac{e_t}{4}} \tag{5.10}$$

5.5 Methods to generate Time Base signals

1. Exponential Circuit

2. UJT Sweep Circuit

3. Miller Circuit

4. Bootstrap Sweep Circuit

5.5.1 Exponential Circuit

Exponential Circuit consists of a resistor, capacitor and a switch. The circuit diagram is shown in the figure 5.4

When the switch is open, capacitor charges exponentially which generate exponential increase sweep. When the switch is closed, capacitor can discharges exponentially if a load is connected thus generating exponential decrease signal which is shown in the figure 5.5

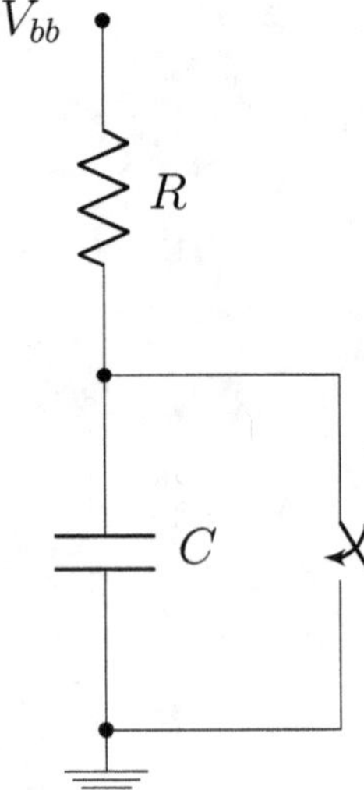

Figure 5.4: Exponential Sweep Circuit

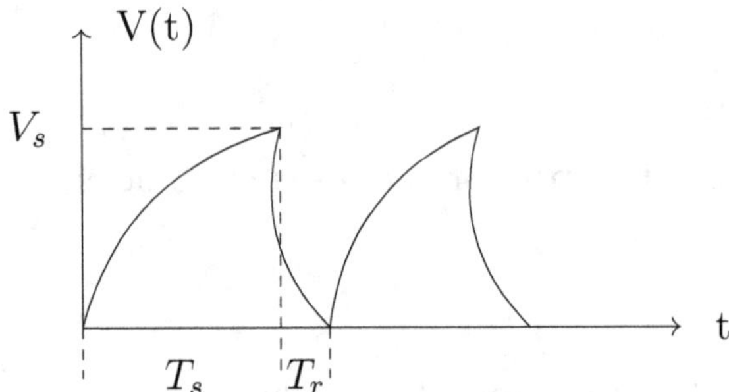

Figure 5.5: Exponential Sweep Circuit output

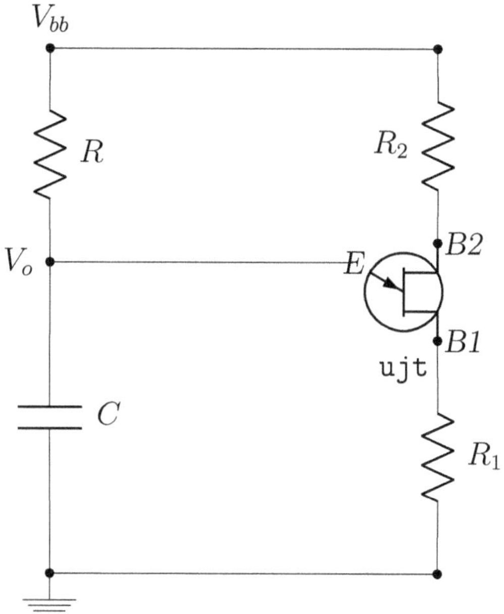

Figure 5.6: UJT Sweep Circuit

5.5.2   UJT Sweep Circuit

The circuit of UJT Sweep Circuit is shown in the figure 5.6. The emitter
of UJT is connected to one end of resistor and capacitor. The Base B_2 is
connected to supply voltage through resistor and B_1 is connected to ground
with resistor.

Equivalent circuit of UJT consists of diode and two resistors is shown in the
figure 5.7. V_p is calculated by taking voltage division rule and is given as

$$V_p = \frac{V_{bb}R_{b1}}{R_{b2} + R_{b1}} \tag{5.11}$$

If diode is practical, cut in voltage of diode is considered and the equation is
modified as

$$V_p = V_\gamma + \frac{V_{bb}R_{b1}}{R_{b2} + R_{b1}} \tag{5.12}$$

$\frac{R_{b1}}{R_{b2}+R_{b1}}$ is constant and equating to η intrinsic stand off ratio.

$$V_p = V_\gamma + \eta V_{bb} \tag{5.13}$$

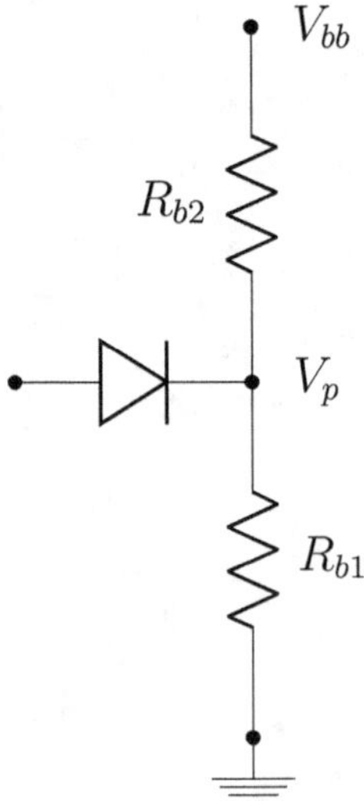

Figure 5.7: Equivalent circuit of UJT

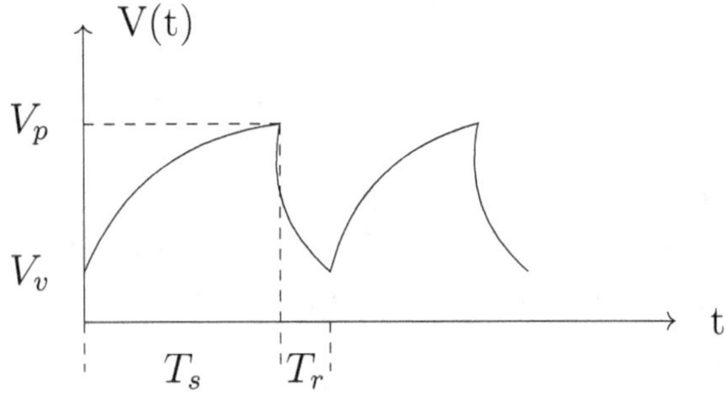

Figure 5.8: UJT Sweep Circuit output

Intially capacitor is uncharged and the voltage across capacitor is zero means UJT is OFF. When a power supply is applied, capacitor starts charging through R. If the voltage across capacitor is $\geq V_p$, UJT is ON. When UJT is ON, capacitor starts discharging. When the voltage across capacitor reaches valley potential V_v, UJT is OFF and again capacitor starts charging. The output waveforms are shown in the figure 5.8

Frequency of oscillations for UJT sweep circuit

Using the basic equation derived from chapter 1 and substituing the values we get

$$V_0 = V_f + (V_i - V_f)e^{-t/RC} \tag{5.14}$$

where V_f is final output voltage and V_i is intiall output voltage.

$$V_p = V_{bb} + (V_v - V_{bb})e^{-t/RC}$$

$$V_p - V_{bb} = +(V_v - V_{bb})e^{-t/RC}$$

$$e^{-t/RC} = \frac{V_p - V_{bb}}{V_v - V_{bb}}$$

$$\frac{-t}{RC} = \ln\left[\frac{V_p - V_{bb}}{V_v - V_{bb}}\right] \tag{5.15}$$

$$t = RC\ln\left[\frac{V_v - V_{bb}}{V_p - V_{bb}}\right]$$

$$= RC\ln\left[\frac{V_{bb} - V_v}{V_{bb} - V_p}\right]$$

since $V_{bb} \gg V_v$,

$$t = RC\ln\left[\frac{V_{bb}}{V_{bb} - V_p}\right] \tag{5.16}$$

Dividing with V_{bb} on both numerator and denominator

$$t = RC\ln\left[\frac{1}{1 - \frac{V_p}{V_{bb}}}\right] \tag{5.17}$$

substituing the expression for V_P and neglecting V_γ, the equation is

$$\boxed{t = RC\ln\left[\frac{1}{1 - \eta}\right]}\ \boxed{f = \frac{1}{t}} \tag{5.18}$$

Problems

1. Calculate the frequency of UJT sweep circuit if the R=10K Ω and C=0.01 μ f, intrinsic stand off ration is 0.8. Calculate sweep time.
 Solution

Given R=10KΩ, C=0.01μf, $\eta = 0.8$. Substituing in the equation

$$t = RC \ln\left[\frac{1}{1-\eta}\right]$$

$$= 100 \times 10^3 \times 0.01 \times 10^{-6} \times \ln\left[\frac{1}{1-0.8}\right]$$

$$= 1.6 \times 10^{-3} sec \tag{5.19}$$

$$f = \frac{1}{t}$$

$$= 621.33 Hz$$

Sweep time $t_s = t - t_r$, where t_r is return time which is very very small and can be neglected also. Assume $t_r = 5\mu s$

$$1.6 \times 10^{-3} = t_s + 5\mu sec$$

$$t_s = 1.59 ms \tag{5.20}$$

2. Design a relaxation oscillator to have 5KHz output frequency using a UJT and 20v power supply. Calculate the sweep amplitude for the circuit shown in the figure 5.6 Consider η=0.7, I_v=1.5ma, I_p=8 μf, $V_{EB}sat$=3v.

Solution Given parameters: η=0.7, I_v=1.5ma, I_p=8 μf, $V_{EB}sat$=3v, f=5KHz, V_{bb}=20. Since there are two different currents, we have to calulate two values of resistance and then considering the average value. One value of resistane during capacitor charging and other while capacitor discharging.

$$R_{max} = \frac{V_{bb} - V_p}{I_p}$$

$$V_p = V_\gamma + \eta V_{bb}$$

$$= 14.6v$$

$$R_{max} = \frac{20 - 14.6}{8 \times \mu}$$

$$= 675K\Omega$$

$$R_{min} = \frac{V_{bb} - V_v}{I_v}$$

$$= \frac{20 - 3}{1.5 \times 10^{-3}}$$

$$= 11.3K\Omega$$

$$R = \frac{R_{max} + R_{min}}{2}$$

$$= 300K\Omega$$

$$t = \frac{1}{f}$$

$$= 0.2msec$$

Assume $t_r=2$ μsec, then $t_s=0.19$msec.

$$t_s = RC\ln[\frac{V_{bb} - V_v}{V_{bb} - V_p}]$$

$$0.19 \times 10^{-3} = (300 \times 10^3)C\ln[\frac{20 - 3}{20 - 14.6}]$$

$$C = 0.55nf$$

Sweep amplitude$=V_p - V_v=11.6$v

(5.21)

(5.22)

3. In UJT sweep circuit R=10KΩ, C=0.1μf, valley potential is 1.5v, $V_{bb}=20$v, cut in voltage of diode is 0.9v, stand off ratio is 0.6. Calulate frequency of oscillations.

Solution Given R=10KΩ, C=0.1μf, V_v 1.5v, V_{bb}=20v, V_γ= 0.9v, η=0.6

$$V_p = V_\gamma + \eta V_{bb}$$
$$= 12.7v$$

$$t_s = RC \ln[\frac{V_{bb} - V_v}{V_{bb} - V_p}] \tag{5.23}$$

$$= 10 \times 10^3 \times 0.1 \times 10^{-6} \times \ln[\frac{20 - 1.5}{20 - 12.7}]$$

$$= 0.9 msec$$
$$f = 1.1 Khz$$

4. A UJT with stand off ratio 0.62 with R=5KΩ, C=0.05μf is used as relaxation oscillator. Determine period, frequency, new value of R which must be changed in order to obtain the frequency of 50Hz. If C is increased by a factor of 10, how the value of R changes if the frequecy is 50Hz.

Solution Given η=0.62 , R=5KΩ, C=0.05μf

(a)

$$t = RC \ln[\frac{1}{1 - \eta}]$$
$$= 0.24 msec \tag{5.24}$$
$$f = 4.1 KHz$$

(b) f=50Hz, t=0.02sec

$$t = RC \ln[\frac{1}{1 - \eta}] \tag{5.25}$$
$$R = 413.4 K\Omega$$

(c) C is increased by a factor of 10

$$t = RC \ln[\frac{1}{1 - \eta}] \tag{5.26}$$
$$R = 41.34 K\Omega$$

5. Design a UJT for sweep amplitude of 10v, sweep time is 1msec, slope error is 10%. Find R_{b1}, R_{b2}

5.6 Basic principle of Miller and Bootstrap Sweep Circuits

By maintaining the current flowing through the capacitor as constant in the basic sweep circuit, the output will be linear sweep signal.

$$V_o(t) = \frac{1}{C} \int_0^t i\,dt$$

$$= \frac{i}{C} \int_0^t 1\,dt \tag{5.27}$$

$$= \frac{i}{C} t$$

$$V_o(t) = \alpha t$$

5.6.1 Miller Sweep Circuit Principle

The basic circuit for Miller Sweep Circuit Principle is shown in the figure 5.9. To make current flowing in the circuit as constant, voltage generator is added whose voltage is equal in magnitude and opposite in sign of the capacitor voltage which is shown in the figure 5.10. The output voltage is taken with reference to the z node as shown in the figure 5.11. The voltage generator is replaced with an amplifier whose gain $= \infty$ as shown in the figure 5.12. The amplifier is replaced with its equivalent circuit as shown in the figure 5.13. Applying Thevenin's equivalent to the input circuit which is shown in the figure 5.14.

$$V' = \frac{VR_i}{R + R_i}$$

$$R' = \frac{RR_i}{R + R_i} \tag{5.28}$$

At $t = 0$, $V_i = 0 = |A|V_i = V_o$, $V_o = 0$ (R_o is neglected)

At $t = \infty$, $V_i = V' = |A|V_i = V_o$, $V_o = 0$ (R_o is neglected)

Slope Error for Miller Sweep Circuit

The slope error is given as

$$e_s = \frac{V_s}{V} \tag{5.29}$$

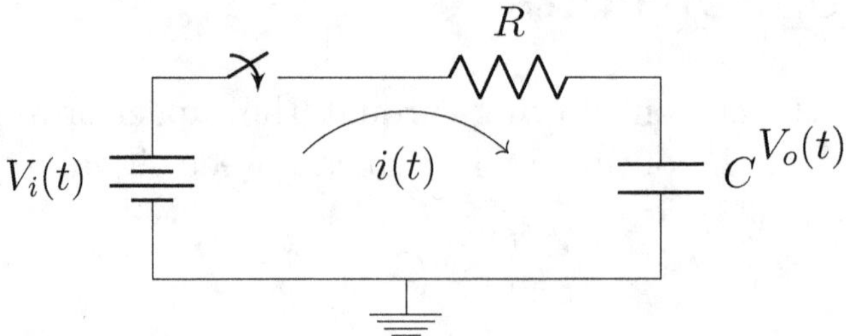

Figure 5.9: Basic Miller Sweep Circuit

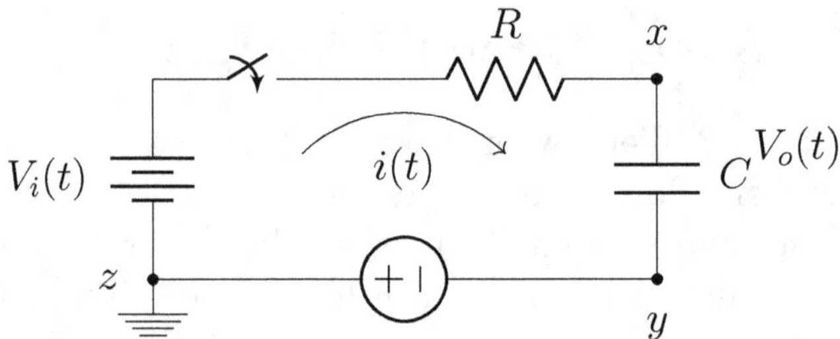

Figure 5.10: Miller sweep with Voltage generator

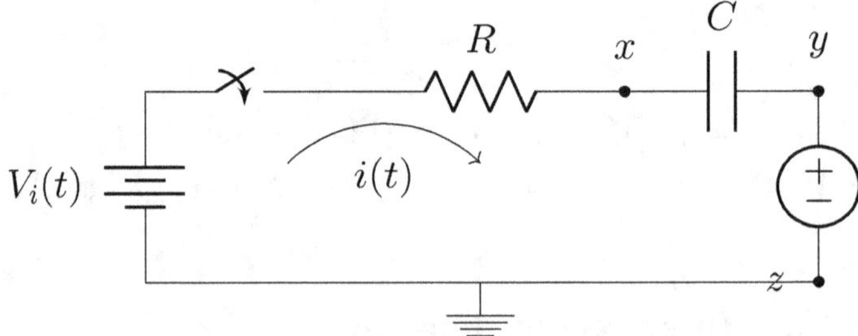

Figure 5.11: with reference z

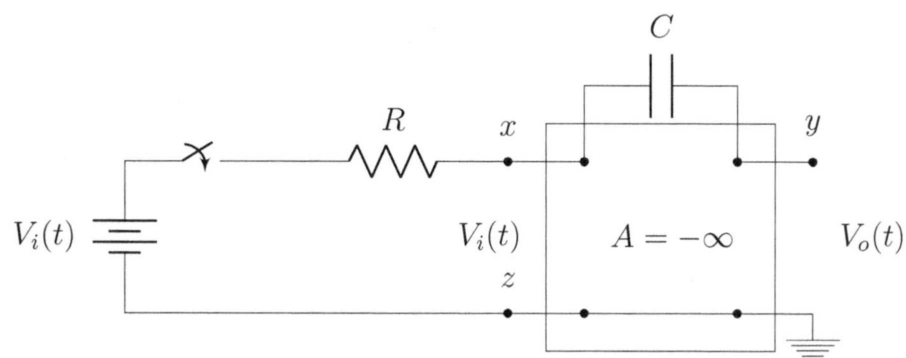

Figure 5.12: with amplifier

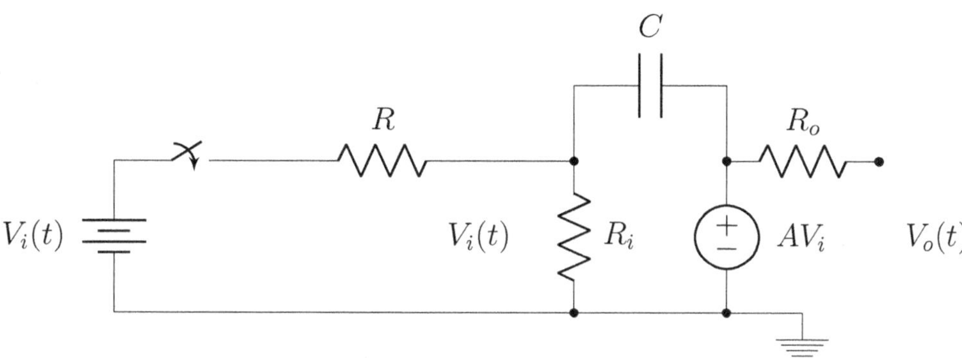

Figure 5.13: Equivalent circuit of amplifier

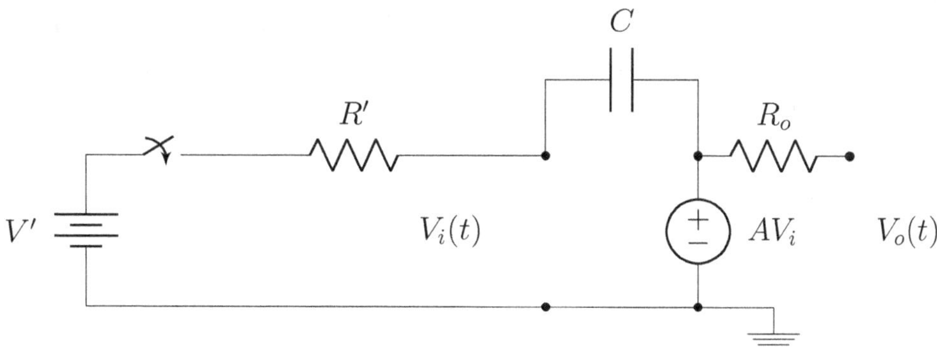

Figure 5.14: Thevenin's Equivalent circuit

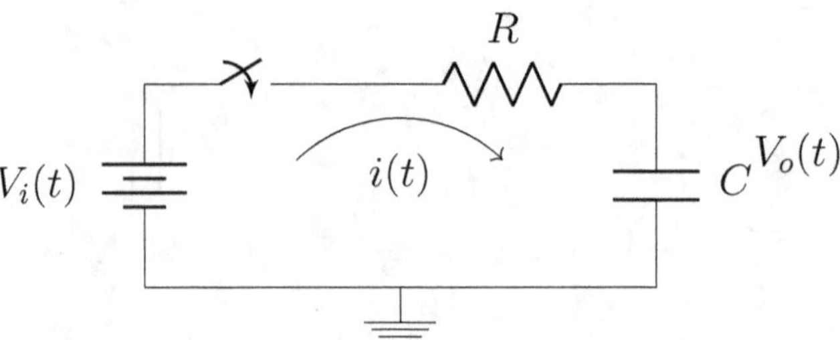

Figure 5.15: Basic Bootstrap Sweep Circuit

where V_s is source or input signal, V is output of the circuit. Substituting we get

$$e_s = \frac{V_s}{|A|V_i}$$

$$= \frac{V_s}{|A|V'} \tag{5.30}$$

$$e_s = \frac{V_s(R + R_i)}{|A|V R_i}$$

5.6.2   Basic Principle of Bootstrap Sweep Circuit

The circuit diagrams of Basic Principle of Bootstrap Sweep Circuit is shown in the figure ??In this bootstrap sweep circuit, node y is consider as the reference which is shown in the figure 5.16. The voltage generator is replaced with an amplifier whose gain is unity and i shown in the figure 5.17. Applying KVL at $t = o$ to the input circuit

$$V - Ri + AV_i - iR_o = v_o \tag{5.31}$$

As capacitor does not charge instantaneously, the voltage across the capacitor is zero. i.e $v_i = 0$

$$V - iR - iR_0 = V_o$$

$$V - V_o = i(R + R_o) \tag{5.32}$$

$$i = \frac{V - V_o}{R + R_o}$$

At time $t = \infty$, applying KVL to the circuit and assuming gain $A = 1$

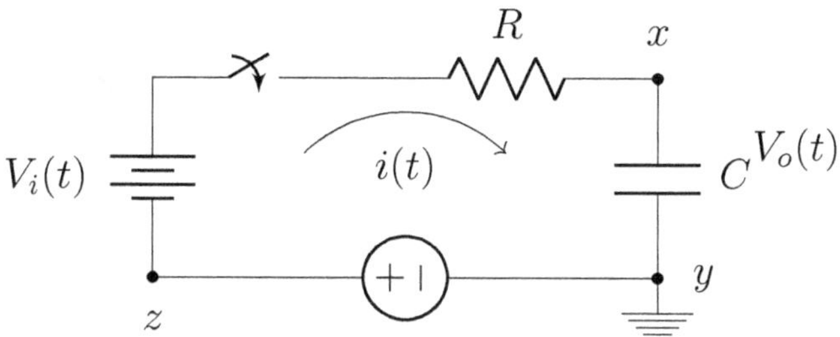

Figure 5.16: with voltage genertor and y as reference

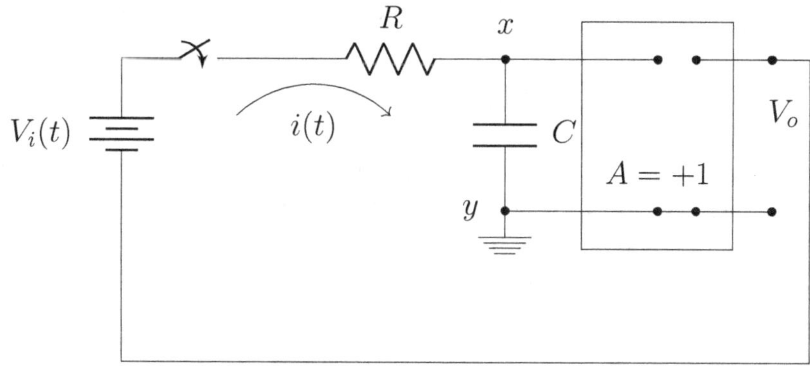

Figure 5.17: with amplifier A=1

$$V - iR - iR_i + AV_i - iR_o = V_o$$
$$V + AV_i - V_o = i(R + R_i + R_o)$$
$$i = \frac{V}{R + R_i}$$
$$V_o = AV_i - iR_o$$
$$V_o = AiR_i - iR_o \tag{5.33}$$
$$V_o = AR_i[\frac{V}{R + R_i}] - R_o[\frac{V}{R + R_i}]$$
$$V_o = \frac{V}{R + R_i}[AR_i - R_o]$$
$$V_o = \frac{V(R_i - R_o)}{R + R_i}$$

Slope Error for Bootstrap Sweep Circuit

The slope error for Bootstrap Sweep Circuit is given as

$$e_s = \frac{V_s}{V}$$
$$= \frac{V_s(R + R_i)}{V(R_i - R_o)} \tag{5.34}$$

5.7   Transistor Miller Sweep Circuit

The circuit diagram of Transistor Miller Sweep Circuit is shown in the figure 5.19. Initially assume transistor T_1 is ON and transistor T_2 is OFF. Then the output voltage $V_o = V_{cc}$. Transistor T_1 acts as a switch and transistor T_2 acts as an amplifier. When T_1 is OFF and transistor T_2 is ON, then the output voltage reduces from V_{cc} following the linear path as shown in the figure 5.18. Thus transistor Miller Sweep Circuit will generate a negative ramp signal.

5.8   Transistorized Bootstrap Sweep Circuit

The bootstrap sweep circuit is shown in the figure 5.20. The boot strap sweep circuit consists of two transistors, transistor T_1 acts as a switch and transistor T_2 acts as an amplifier. When transistor T_1 is OFF, the capacitor C_1 charges through the supply voltage V_{cc} and diode D.When a negative

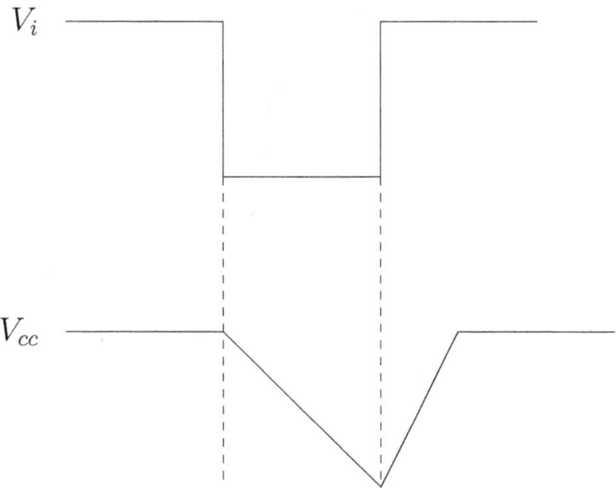

Figure 5.18: Wave forms of Transistor Miller Sweep Circuit

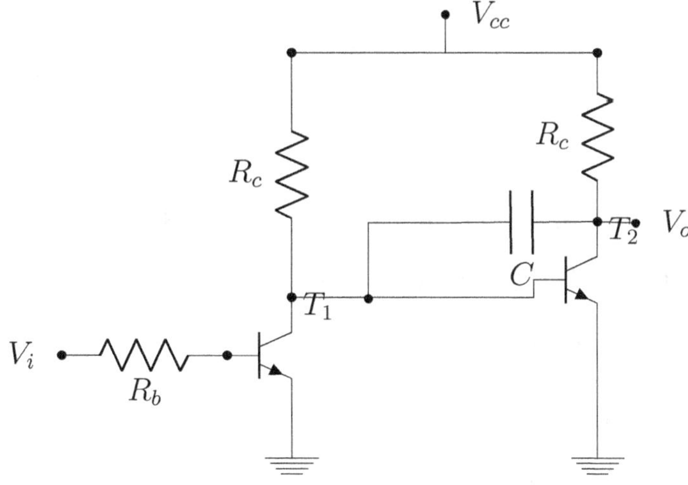

Figure 5.19: Transistor Miller Sweep Circuit

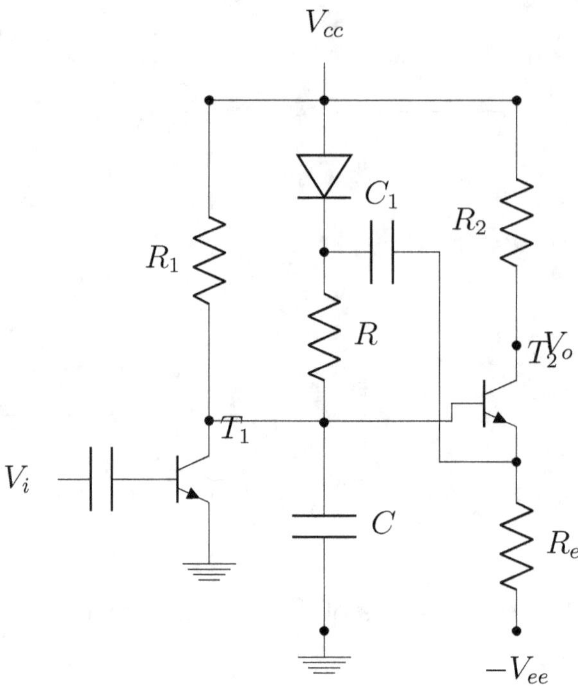

Figure 5.20: Transistorized Bootstrap Sweep Circuit

triggering voltage is applied base of transistor T_1, T_1 will be OFF. Now the capacitor C_1 discharges while making the capacitor C charges. During this the diode D is reverse biased. Thus the circuit produces a positive ramp signal which is shown in the figure 5.21.

5.9 Differences between Miller and Bootstrap Time Base Generators

Miller Time Base Generators

1. It generates negative ramp voltage wrt time.

2. It uses inverting amplifier.

3. Gain $= \infty$.

4. High input impedance is not required.

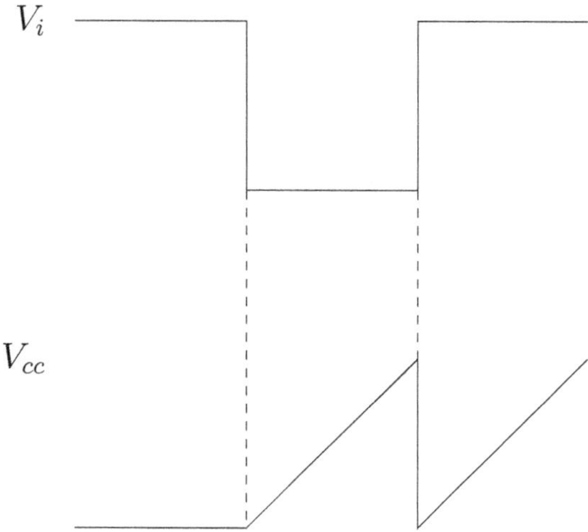

Figure 5.21: Wave forms of Bootstrap Sweep Circuit

Bootstrap Time Base Generator

1. It generates positive ramp voltage wrt time.

2. It uses non-inverting amplifier.

3. Gain = 1.

4. High input impedance is required.

Chapter 6

Sampling Gates

A circuit whose output is equal to input for a period of time and zero or independent of input for remaining period of time is called a Sampling Gate. A gate or control signal is used in designing a Sampling gate. The period during which the output is equal to input is called as Transmission Period $(T_x P)$ otherwise it is non-transmission period $(non - T_x P)$.

6.1 Basic Sampling Gate

The circuit diagram of basic sampling gate is shown in the figure 6.1. The circuit consists of a switch, Resistor and voltage supply.

When the switch is closed, the circuit acts as closed circuit. Then the output voltage $V_o(t) = V_i(t)$. When the switch is open, the circuit acts as open circuit. Then the output voltage $V_o(t) = 0$.

Figure 6.1(b) shows the switch is in series with the supply voltage. When the the switch is closed, the circuit, the circuit acts as open circuit. Then the output voltage $V_o(t) = V_i(t)$.

6.2 Unidirectional Sampling Gates

In nidirectional Sampling Gates, switch is replaced with a diode. The circuit diagram of Unidirectional Sampling Gates is shown in the figure 6.2. $V_i(t)$ is

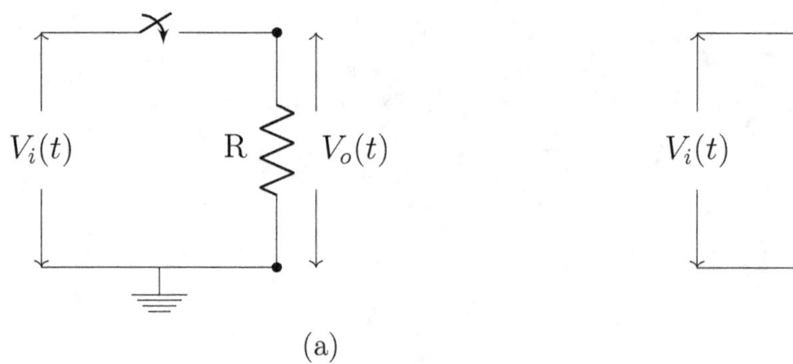

Figure 6.1: Basic Sampling Gate:(a) Switch is in series with supply votage (b) Switch is in parallel with supply votage

the input pulse signal and $V_g(t)$ is a gate signal which is a rectangular pulse. $-V_1$ and $-V_2$ are the voltage levels of gate signal.

The anlaysis of the circuit is based on transmission period and non-transmission period. Let when $V_g(t)=-V_1$, the circuit acts as transmission period and $V_g(t)=-V_2$, the circuit acts as non-transmission period. The conditions to make circuit to allow input at ouput i.e transmission period is given as $V_p = V_i + |V_1| > 0$. To satisfy this condition, the input voltage $V_i > |V_1|$. During this period, the diode acts as short circuit. Then the output is proportional to the input. V_p is the voltage at anode of diode i.e $V_i(t) + V_g(t)$.

To maintain non-transmission period, $V_p = V_i + |V_2| < 0$. To satisfy this condition, the input voltage $|V_2| > V_i$. During this period, the diode acts as open circuit. Then the output is zero.

Assume the input signal $V_i(t)$ is 10v pulse signal, $V_2 = -20$ and V_1 is variable. The output waveforms for different values of V_1 is shown in the figure 6.3

- When $V_1 = -10$, the output voltage $V_o(t) = 0$

- When $V_1 = -50$, the output voltage $V_o(t) = 5$

- When $V_1 = 0$, the output voltage $V_o(t) = 10$

- When $V_1 = 5$, the output voltage $V_o(t) = 15$

During the last case, the output is 15v which is greater than the input signal. The difference of the input voltage and measured voltage is called as

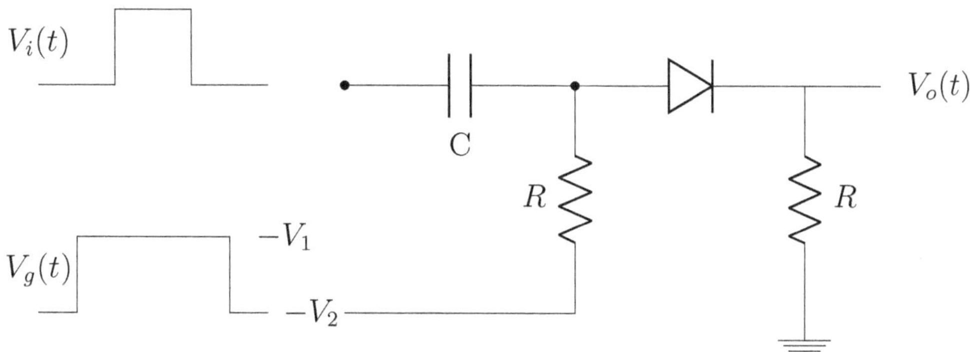

Figure 6.2: Unidirectional Sampling Gate

Pedestal.

6.3 Unidirectional Sampling gate with more than one input signal

In this circuit we consider more than one input signal is applied to sampling gate with one gate signal. The circuit diagram is shown in the figure 6.4 In this circuit diagram 6.4, the gate signal is connected as common to both the input signal. Let V_{p1} is the voltage at diode D_1 and V_{p2} is the voltage at diode D_2 Two input signals are connected to both the anodes of diode. To design the non-transmission period, the condition to satisfy is $V_{p1} = V_1(t) + |V_2| < 0$ keeping $|V_2| > V_1(t)$ and $V_{p2} = V_2 + |V1| < 0$ keeping $|V_2| > V_2(t)$.

To design the transmission period, the condition to satisfy is $V_{p1} = V_1(t) + |V_1| > 0$ keeping $V_1(t) > |V_1|$ and $V_{p2} = V_2(t) + |V1| > 0$ keeping $V_2(t) > V_1$.The gate signal effects the transmission period since it is applied simultaneously to both the diodes. This effect is called **Loding Effect**.

6.4 Unidirectional Sampling gate which reduces loading effect

When the gate signal is applied simultaneously to both the diodes, only one diode may conduct in transmission period. To reduce this loading effect, the

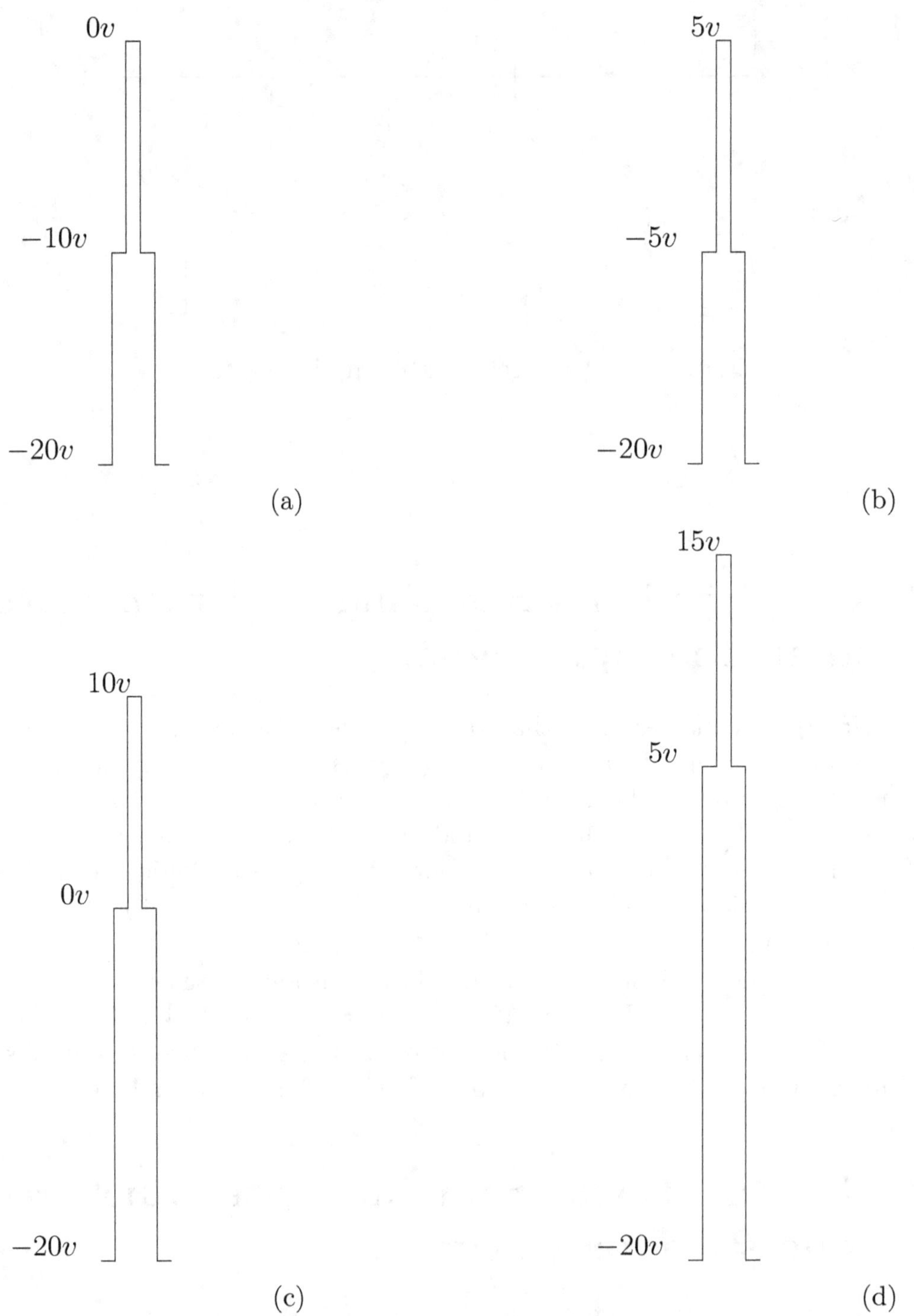

Figure 6.3: Unidirectional Sampling Gate:(a) $V_1 = -10$, the output voltage $V_o(t) = 0$ (b) $V_1 = -50$, the output voltage $V_o(t) = 5$ (c) $V_1 = 0$, the output voltage $V_o(t) = 10$ (d)$V_1 = 5$, the output voltage $V_o(t) = 15$

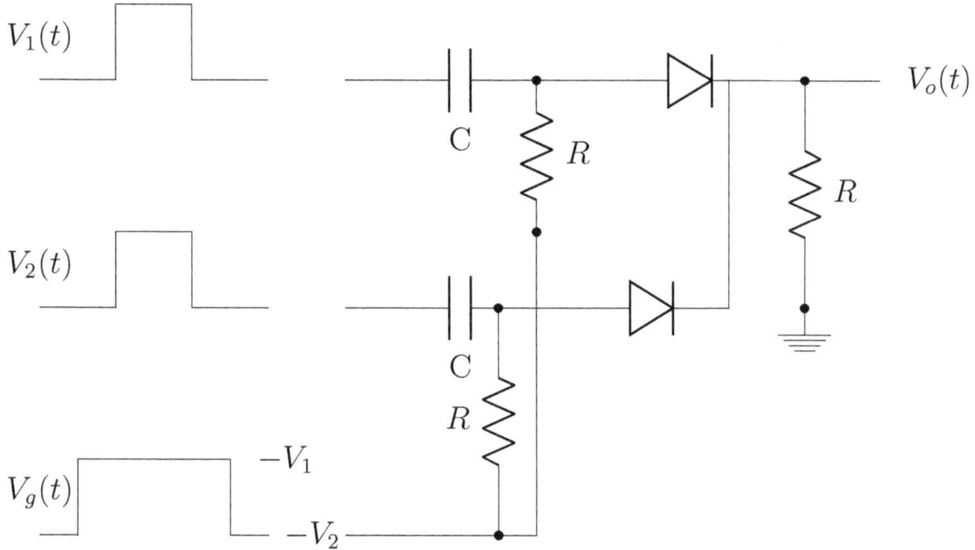

Figure 6.4: Unidirectional Sampling gate with more than one input signal

circuit is modified which is shown in the figure 6.5

6.5 Bidirectional Sampling gate using transistor

The circuit diagram of Bidirectional Sampling gate using transistor is shown in the figure 6.6. Here transistor is operated in cut off and active region only. In cut off region, the output is independent of input. In active region, the output is dependent of input. Both the input and gate signal is applied to base of the npn transistor. During transmission period, transistor operates in active region. The conditions for transmission period are $V_s + |V_1| > V_{BE}$ and $V_s > |V_1|$. Then the output V_o is 180 degree phase shift of the input signal which is shown in the figure 6.7. When the input signal is zero, then $V_o = V_{CC} - I_c R_c$. For non-transmission period, transistors operates in cut off. The conditions are $V_s + |V_2| < V_{BE}$ and $|V_2| > V_s$. Then the output $V_o = V_{cc}$ which is shown in the figure 6.7.

If the output during non transmission period is equal to the output during transmission period when the input signal is zero, then there is no pedestal.

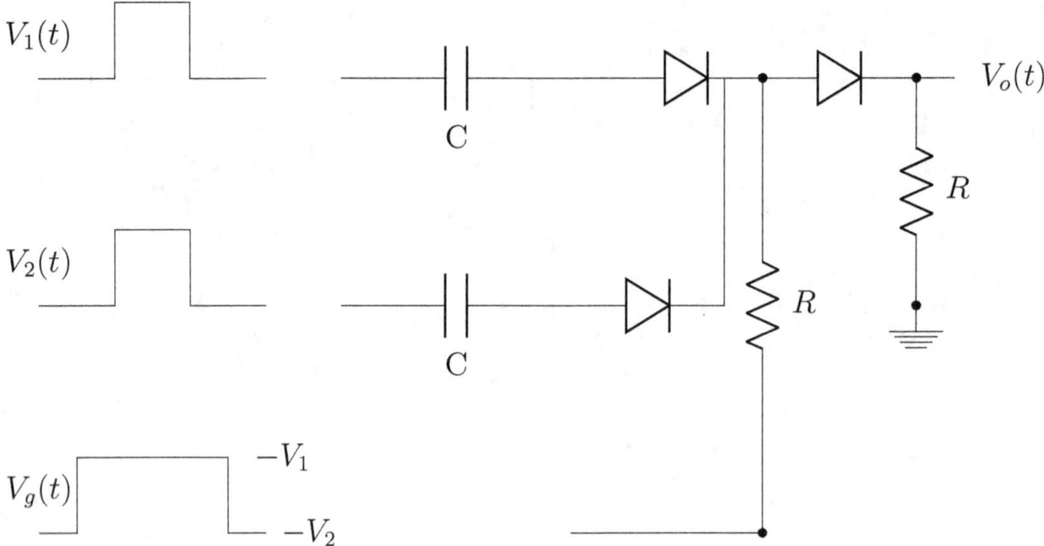

Figure 6.5: Unidirectional Sampling gate with more than one input signal which reduces loading effect

If not, there exists pedestal. Pedestal are of two types. **Positive pedestal:** If the output during non transmission period is **Negative pdestal:** If the output during non transmission period is less than the output during transmission period when the input signal is zero.

6.6   Reduction of pedestal

Pedestal in Bidirectional Sampling gate using transistor is reduced by using one more transistor and considering two gate signals which are opposite in nature. The circuit diagram is shown in the figure 6.8 and the waveforms are shown in the figure 6.9. For non transmission period, $V_s + V_{c1} < 0.7$. Then transsistor T_1 is OFF and transistor T_2 is ON. The output voltage $V_o = V_{cc} - I_c R_c$.

For transmission period, $V_s + V_{c1} > 0.7$. Then transsistor T_1 is ON and transistor T_2 is OFF. The ouptut V_o is 180 degree phase shift of input signal. If the input signal is zero, then $V_o = V_{cc} - I_c R_c$. So pedestal is reduced.

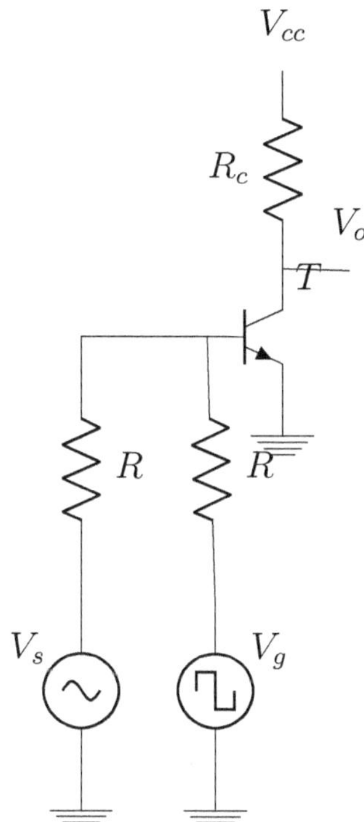

Figure 6.6: Bidirectional Sampling gate using transistor

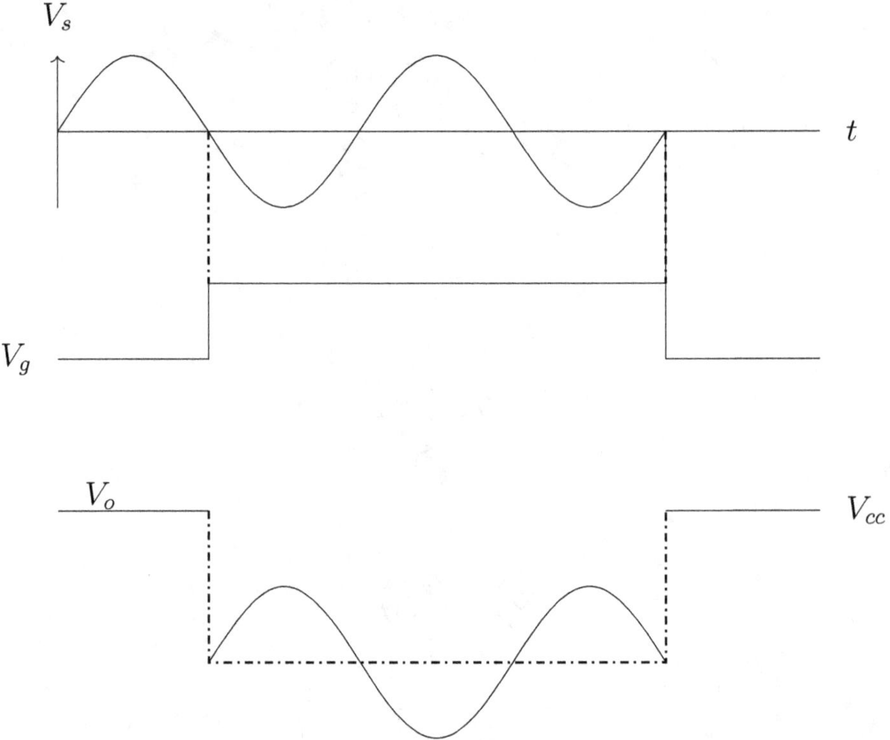

Figure 6.7: Waveforms of Bidirectional Sampling gate using transistor

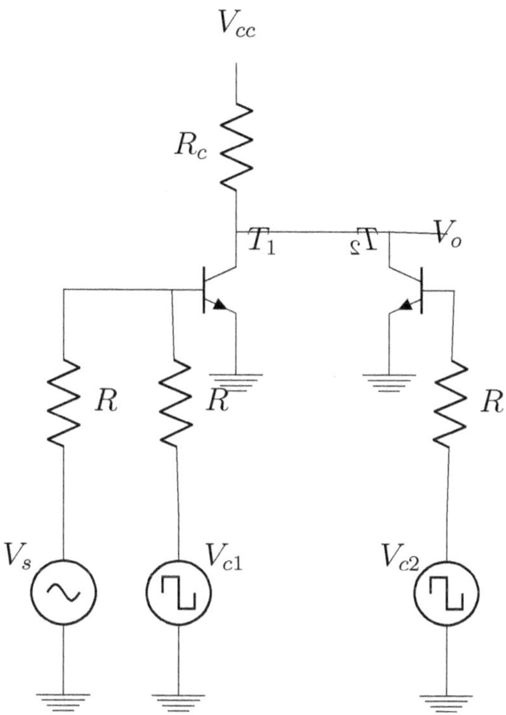

Figure 6.8: Reduction of pedestal

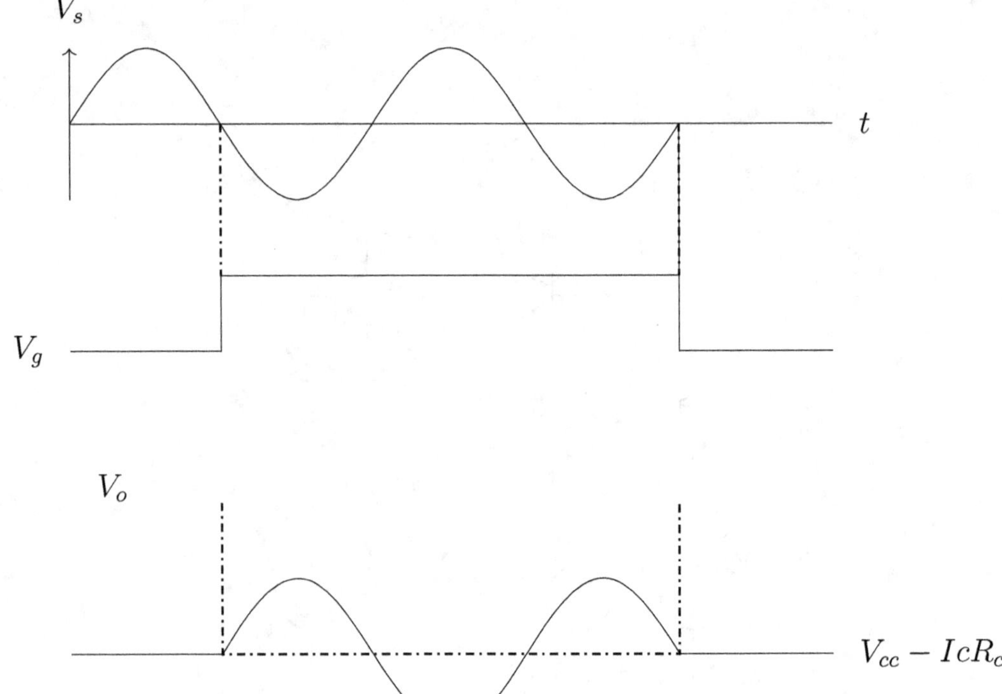

Figure 6.9: Waveforms: Reduction of pedestal

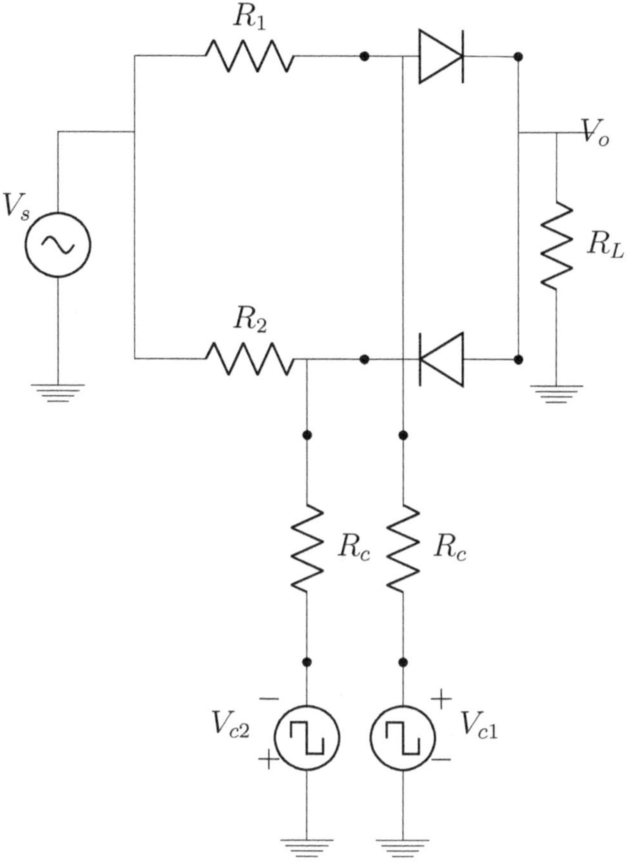

Figure 6.10: Two diode bidirectional sampling gate

6.7 Two diode bidirectional sampling gate

The circuit diagram of Two diode bidirectional sampling gate is shown in the figure 6.10.

For transmission period both the diodes acts as forward biased and for non transmission period, both the diodes acts as reverse biased. The conditions of transmission period $V_a = V_s + V_c > 0$ and $V_b = V_s + V_c < 0$.

The conditions of non transmission period $V_a = V_s + V_n >< 0$ and $V_b = V_s + V_{cn} > 0$. The circuit is reaaranged and shown in the figure 6.11. Applying thevenin's theorem for both the sides which is shown in the figure 6.12

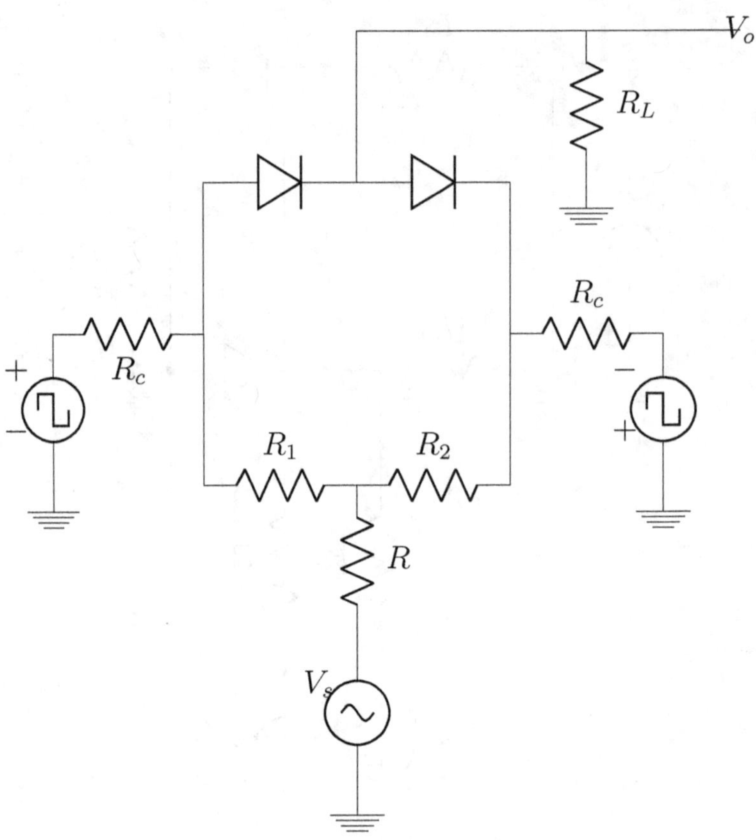

Figure 6.11: Rearranged Two diode bidirectional sampling gate

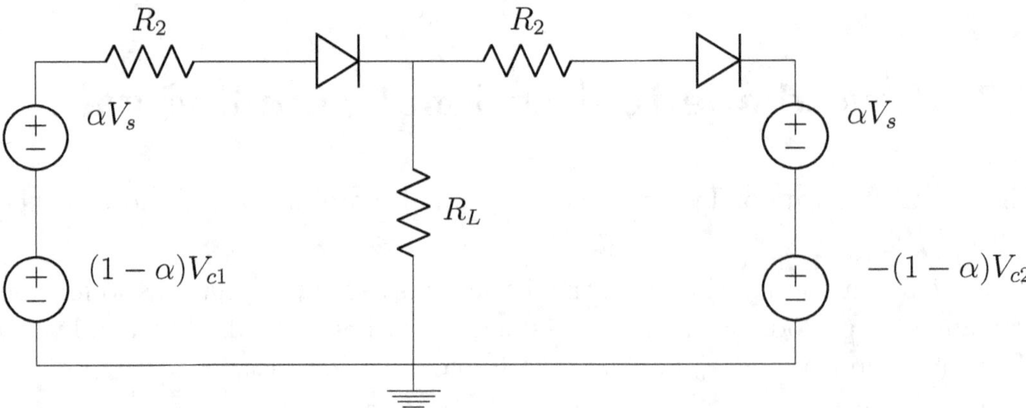

Figure 6.12: Thevenin's equivalent Two diode bidirectional sampling gate

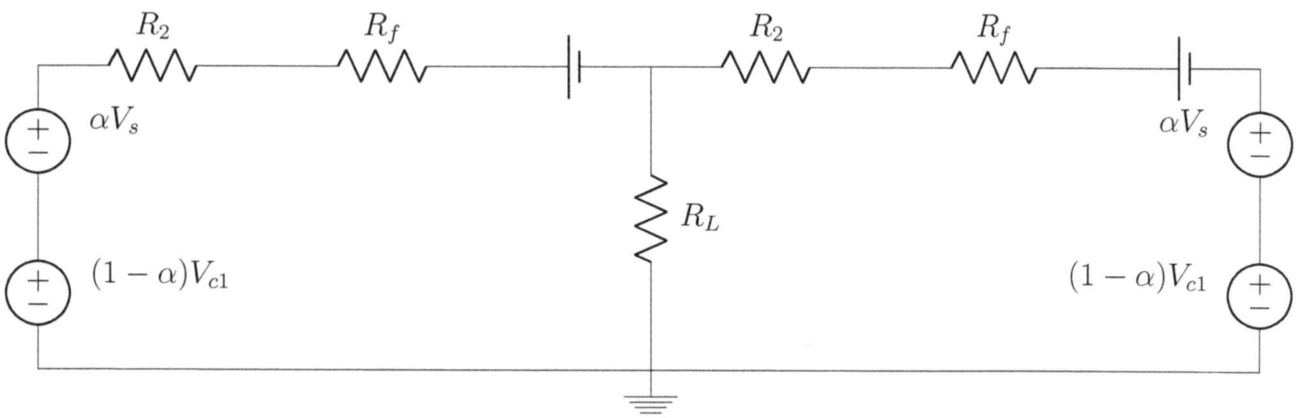

Figure 6.13: Replacing diodes of Two diode bidirectional sampling gate

If $V_{c1} = 0$,

$$V_{RC} = \frac{V_s \times R_c}{R_1 + R_c} \tag{6.1}$$

Let $\alpha = \frac{R_c}{R_1 + R_c}$

Then $V_{RC} = \alpha V_s$

If $V_s = 0$,

$$V_{RC} = \frac{V_{c1} \times R_1}{R_1 + R_c} \tag{6.2}$$

Then $V_{RC} = V_{c1}(1 - \alpha)$

Thevenin's resistance $R_{th} = R_c // R_1 = R_2$

Replacing the diodes with linear piece wise model which is shown in the figure 6.13.

Neglecting V_γ and assuming $R_2 + R_f = R_3$.

Applying thevenin's theorem for both the sides, the circuit is shown in the figure 6.14 the output is given as

$$V_o = \frac{\alpha v_s \times R_L}{R_L + R_3/2} \tag{6.3}$$

6.8 Applications of Sampling gates

1. Multiplexers

2. Digital to Analog converters

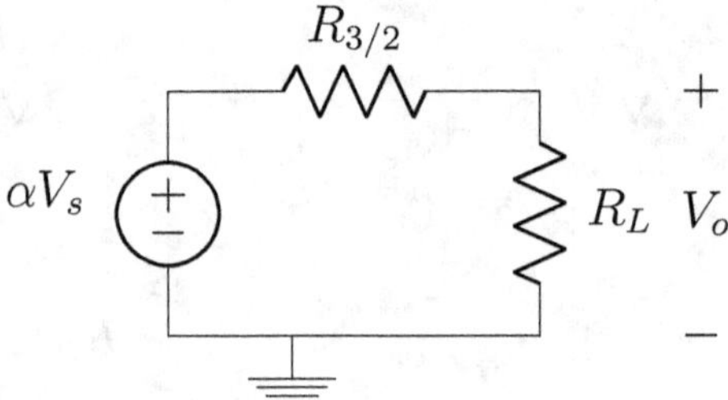

Figure 6.14: Simplified circuit of Two diode bidirectional sampling gate

3. Chopper Amplifier

4. Sample and Hold circuit

5. Sampling scope